Decorative Painting

Painting
Folk Art
Flowers

with
Enid Hoessinger

NORTH LIGHT BOOKS
CINCINNATI, OHIO

ABOUT THE AUTHOR

Enid's interest in art was evident from an early age, when she began painting and sketching. Her travels to Europe in later years sparked her interest in traditional folk art and the painting styles of master furniture painters of the past.

In 1976, Enid developed her now-so-successful thirteen brushstrokes and multi-loading techniques to simplify teaching the various folk art styles and motifs. She teaches her techniques throughout her homeland of Australia, as well as in many countries throughout the world.

Enid joined the Society of Decorative Painters in 1991 and became a Certified Decorative Artist in 1995.

Other fine North Light Books are available from your local bookstore, art supply store or direct from the publisher.

03 02 01 00   5 4 3 2

Library of Congress Cataloging-in-Publication Data

Hoessinger, Enid.
    Painting folk art flowers with Enid Hoessinger.
        p.   cm.
    ISBN 0-89134-889-1 (pbk.: alk. paper).—ISBN 0-89134-943-X (alk. paper)
    1. Flowers in art. 2. Folk art. 3. Painting—Technique. I. Title.
ND1400.H57   1999
751.4'26—dc21

98-41457
CIP

Editors: Kathryn Kipp and Jennifer Long
Production editors: Michelle Kramer and Nicole R. Klungle
Designer: Mary Barnes Clark
Production coordinator: Kristen D. Heller

DEDICATION

I dedicate this book to my loving husband and family;

to my dear friend Anna-Liisa Buchholtz, who has always respected the originality of my teachings;

and to all those who have said "But I can't do that!" and have then done it anyway.

ACKNOWLEDGMENTS

Reflecting on the years since I started painting, there are so many people who have influenced me and many events have led up to the success of the multi-loading technique. I thank God for granting me a talent before I even gave it a thought. I thank my parents for their encouragement throughout the years and for that first painting set.

Joe, my Austrian husband, shared that first painting set when we met, proving his wonderful artistic skills. His support and appreciation for even the least of my work made it a joy. When my interest in European folk art steered me into teaching, Joe further encouraged me by designing and making all the woodwork I needed— and he still does today. His natural flair and ability in the trade he learned as a boy shows through his work, from the simplest to the most exquisite handcarved articles and furniture. His interest in photography as a hobby has not been wasted: He is responsible for most of the pictures in this book. Joe, your help is very much appreciated.

My sincere thanks to my daughter Theresa, mother of our three precious grandchildren, who made time in her busy schedule to be my right hand and help me with the initial editing of this book.

The chapter of the Women's Association affiliated to Associated Country Women of the World must take responsibility for initiating my teaching career: Marianne Lucouw, the president at the time, succeeded in talking me into sharing my then-untrained skills with their members. Thank you for the part you played.

I think of master furniture painters of bygone eras whose collective works influenced me and inspired my incessant development of new methods and effects with the brush. I am sure they are smiling down on us all with pride.

The search for my perfect brush ended when I approached Habico Company, who designed, adapted and continues to monitor my brushes to ensure they remain of the highest quality.

Without students, I would not have needed to develop the multi-loading technique. Their devotion and wonderful efforts are what spurred me on to give them more and take them further. "Your wish was my command," wasn't it you, Veronika Ricketson? Thank you each and every one of you; the days of struggling with Tölzer roses paid off!

A highlight of my decorative painting career came in 1991, when I became a member of the National Society of Decorative Painters. At my first attendance, I was overwhelmed by and inspired to see the tremendous hive of activity and the uniqueness of various decorative artists. Through this experience, I was encouraged to exhibit and teach at their annual conventions. If it weren't for my attendance at the conventions, I would not have been approached by DecoArt, who put an end to my search for paints suited to my needs. Thank you, Stan. You and your team did it well.

Last but not least, editor Kathy Kipp, who also approached me at a convention, and offered the enthusiasm that inspired me to bring this book to fruition. Her help in guiding me over this long distance has been greatly appreciated. I could not imagine doing it without her. Thank you to North Light Books for giving me this opportunity to share my technique with others.

Table of Contents

Introduction

Folk art is an "umbrella" description, covering the art forms of many nations. It refers mostly to unskilled expressions of thoughts and emotions, often naive in design, that record the everyday things around the artist. I see authentic folk art pieces as photo albums of the past. Original folk art has a certain simple charm about it. It's not easy to capture the innocence of this early work, even when copying it.

Folk art has a vast history that would be impossible to cover in one book. Historians recording the folklore of their respective regions over the past century have written many, many resource books. If you're interested in learning more about the origins of folk art, check your local library.

When I started painting folk art in South Africa in 1976, fellow members of an association in adult education urged me to teach them the Bauernmalerei designs I did. It was here that I first combined the now-so-efficient thirteen brushstrokes with the technique of multi-loading the brush. (At right is the first piece I painted.) To remain true to the art form, I drew my inspiration for designs from traditional publications available only in German. Because of the success of these classes, which started off merely as a simple sharing of skills, some of these members asked to continue on a paying basis. So I continued to teach my techniques.

As my students developed their skills, they wanted to learn more. My incessant research paid off—I was ready to help them progress. While the demand for my techniques continues to grow, I never change my teaching method, because it produces such a high success rate.

In 1981 we moved from South Africa—my country of birth—to Cairns, Queensland, Australia. I now had to start from the beginning with forty-eight new students. In my spare time, I painted furniture for myself, recording the different eras of folk art. In 1987 I was invited to teach in the southern part of Australia, where I held five-day seminars, rather than one lesson per week, which produced incredible results.

During the past years I've taught people with previously attained artistic skills; their demands inspired me to bring them something more than traditional folk art, which will always have a place in interior decoration and a special place in my heart. It was at this time that I directed my teaching to brush technique rather than a particular art form. As my students progress, I now include more refined and realistic designs in my teaching, still using the same multi-loading technique. It is this technique that I bring to you in this book.

It has been, and always will be, my wish to help those who want to create beauty around them and need help to do so. Some claim they do not possess the slightest bit of artistic ability. However, as long as they want to learn, I prove these students wrong—many of them become proficient painters and teachers. For the realistic artist, this technique has become a wonderful tool to create detail that otherwise is a tedious task.

Besides this book being a teaching manual of my multi-loading technique for painting flowers, it contains eight practical, step-by-step projects. The designs for these projects were inspired and extracted from this traditional 1788 *schrank* (the German word for armoire) from Bavaria. Each project will note from which part of the schrank I took the inspiration for that design. This is just a small sampling of the unlimited design variations possible. Extract and re-arrange individual flowers or sections of the patterns provided in this book to create your own designs.

It is important to follow the instructions in this book from the beginning, using this book as a "teacher in your home." Every aspect of my thirteen-brushstroke multi-loading technique is thoroughly covered, with a special section showing common problems and how to fix them. I feel sure this book will give you great pleasure. Enjoy using my multi-loading technique as you paint the designs within. ☞

Chapter One

Brushes

Natural Sable Rounds

The multi-loading technique taught in this book requires a specific tool: a natural sable round brush. It's very important you use natural sable brushes for my technique, because:

• The downward scales allow the paint to flow forward to the tip naturally, enabling you to cover more distance with one loading.

• When applying pressure, the brush does not spread out of control.

• The brush has a reasonable amount of elasticity, making for controlled bounce-back.

• When the brush is flattened to a knife-edge, it remains in this shape for multiple small strokes and facilitates reloading.

Only a round brush has multiple "sides," giving it great potential for layering colors. Because the brush is not limited to one side, the various facets of the brush can be used to grade color from lighter to darker as required. A round brush can also retain more paint for continuous use.

There are scores of different brands of brushes to choose from: Just be sure the brushes you choose are natural sable. I can recommend the following brushes because they have been adapted to suit my technique:

• Habico 122AF no. 3 and no. 4 (made of pure sable)

My most frequently used Habico brushes.

• Habico 110F no. 3 and no. 4 (made of Kolinsky sable)

• Habico 108AF no. 3 and no. 4 (designed for my technique; made of pure sable)

• Habico 122A no. 5 (used on occasion)

Start off with series 122AF brushes, which are less expensive, until you feel ready to upgrade to the higher quality 110F brushes. The 108AF brushes are perfect for traveling.

I recommend purchasing a no. 3 and a no. 4 brush, since these are required for my technique. While I automatically reach for a no. 3, larger elements may require a no. 4.

Other Brushes

For profiled edges, the best brushes are Habico series 356 no. 6, no. 8 and no. 12 (or the equivalent brushes in another brand). These brushes are ox-hair lettering brushes. You will not believe the time you save!

Caring for Your Brushes

The downward scales of natural hair will allow the acrylic particles to flush out when cleaning it. Therefore it does not matter if the brush is loaded up to the metal ferrule with paint. It is the manner of cleaning the brush that is important. When you're finished painting, use clean water to rinse the brush. If you wish, you may use a brush cleaner, but rinse the brush thoroughly.

The Don'ts of Brush Care

• **Don't** scrub your brushes in brush basins—you can break the hairs off at the ferrule.

• **Don't** dry brushes by pinching them between your fingers—this is a bad habit!

• **Don't** scrub the brush when mixing colors. Instead, pull the brush away from the point.

• **Don't** mash the heel of the brush down while painting. This action will bruise the hair around the metal ferrule, weakening the hair's elasticity.

• **Don't** leave paint to dry in the brush.

• **Don't** leave the brush standing in a container of water.

• **Don't** paint on abrasive surfaces—it wears off the hair at the heel of the brush.

1 Tap the brush against the side of the jar.

2 Dry the brush by pulling it horizontally over the surface of a paper towel to remove any excess moisture and drops accumulating along the metal ferrule. Do *not* pinch the brush between your fingers.

The "Buchholtz Bottle"

Recycled plastic bottles work very well as water containers, because they can be used again. Merely cut the top off at the required length and cut a notch on the edge to provide a place for your brush. Thank you, Anna-Liisa, for this tip!

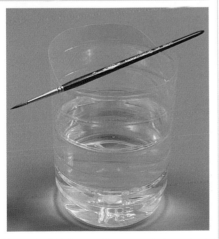

Chapter Two

Paint and Palette

Paint

I require only ten colors of DecoArt Americana acrylic paint to create my folk art designs. There are three primary colors: Brilliant Red DA145, Yellow Light DA144 and True Blue DA36, and three specially mixed colors: Antique Gold Deep DA146, Antique Green DA147 and Oxblood DA139. These are supplemented by Titanium White DA1, Lamp Black DA67, Burnt Umber DA64 and Blue Green DA142. Any additional colors are used for backgrounds and are indicated in the individual projects.

When using my techniques, it is extremely important that the white is adjusted by adding 1 teaspoon of distilled water per 2 oz. bottle. Shake this mixture well.

Preparing Your Palette

Enid's User-Friendly Wet Palette is designed to keep our environment safe and can be used in all climates. To make your own, look for bakers' parchment—it does not impart any greasy residue and keeps the moisture in, preventing the paint from drying on the surface. Use a sheet of *white* absorbent paper towel (colored surfaces hinder accurate color mixing).

1 Fold the paper towel and parchment in half; place the folded paper towel inside.

2 Fold the longest side over twice, pressing down firmly. Fold the corners of the ends and then repeat the process on the opposite side. (Pretend the paper towel is a gift you're wrapping with parchment.)

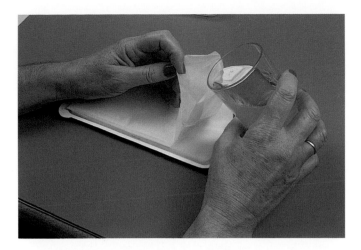

3 When you're ready to paint, open one end of the parchment and place the heel of your hand down on the other end. Now pour enough water into the parchment to saturate the paper towel.

4 Push out all the air bubbles, fold the flaps back and place the palette onto the lid of a plastic container, folds down. Put the base of the container upside down over the top to cover the palette when it is not in use. That's all there is to making a palette.

Materials List

- Habico Brush 122AF—no. 3, no. 4, no. 5
- Habico Brush 110F—no. 3, no. 4
- Habico Brush 108AF—no. 3, no. 4
- Habico Brush 356—no. 6, no. 8, no. 10, no. 12
- Habico Brush 204AK—no. 20
- Soft varnish brush
- Bristle brush for oil paint
- DecoArt Americana acrylic paints
- Water-based varnish
- Sandpaper
- DecoArt Matte spray sealer
- Tracing paper
- Greaseproof paper
- Paper towels
- Graphite-Saral Paper
- Black graphite pencil
- Stylus
- Pencil
- Eraser
- Masking tape
- Winsor & Newton Burnt Umber oil paint
- Saucer
- Palette
- Old soft cloths (*lint-free*)
- Gloves
- Refined linseed oil
- Pure gum turps (distilled or natural)
- Water jar
- Wooden surfaces of your choice

Tips

- On dry days, moisture dissipates from the paper towel and air pockets form inside the parchment, causing the paint to dry on the surface. Open one end, top-up with clean water and allow the air to escape so that the parchment paper is in contact with the wet paper towel inside.
- When the palette is not in use, place the cover on. To transport, close the lid. In very dry climates, adjust by adding a little more water.
- Use both sides of the palette before discarding it. Place a piece of paper on the used side, turn it over, reverse the folds and give it a drink—and have one for yourself—you'll both be as good as new.
- This type of palette can be made anywhere and in any size. Make up lots of them when you have some spare time.

Chapter Three

The Thirteen Basic Brushstrokes

I designed these brushstrokes specifically to teach brush control, particularly for people who don't know where to start. The control of pressure and lift is the first requirement of my technique and must be mastered before multi-loading the brush.

Brushstrokes are frequently used by themselves; brushstrokes one, two and three, in particular, are used at an elementary level. Strokes can also be combined; e.g., brushstrokes four and six, five and seven, eight and nine, and eight, nine and ten, which are chiefly used for rose or similar-shaped leaves. I call my thirteen brushstrokes the "painting alphabet." They *must* be painted exactly as I have demonstrated. Yet, as with the reading alphabet, the A in a word like *apple* is pronounced with a short sound, not as it stands on its own; so, too, many of my brushstrokes are "pronounced" differently. For example, the S-stroke is a weakened form of brushstrokes four, five, six and seven. Sometimes we may only require part of one stroke and combine it with another, as for a tulip. Combinations of strokes eleven, twelve and thirteen, which produce a host of different types of flowers, will complete the alphabet needed to paint confidently, and relate it to different shapes and objects.

All brushstrokes can be painted in different sizes with the same brush, depending on the amount of pressure applied. For larger strokes the brush lays at a 45° angle and more pressure is applied; smaller strokes use a steeper angle and less pressure. The lift is the same for all strokes, with short or long tails as required. Try not to exert pressure *on* the heel of the brush; instead, exert pressure *toward* the heel. Follow through slowly and examine each action.

I initially designed these strokes to create form for elementary work (left). However, by repeating and practicing these strokes you will develop brush control. The brushstrokes can be adapted to paint any flower, allowing skilled artists to use the brushstrokes for optimum effect without being obvious (below).

Brush Exercise

Try this with a clean, dry brush. Unless otherwise stated in the following strokes, the brush should rest comfortably at a 45° angle to the surface to start the strokes. This will allow the hairs to splay apart, which is necessary for gradation when the brush is loaded with more than one color. Do not lead the brush; allow it to do the work. Merely apply pressure and pull your fingers back into your palm as if catching a thread and pulling it through the eye of a needle. Do not roll the brush unless instructed.

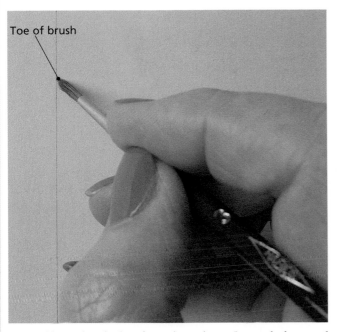

Toe of brush

1 Hold your hand relaxed, touching the surface with the toe of the brush.

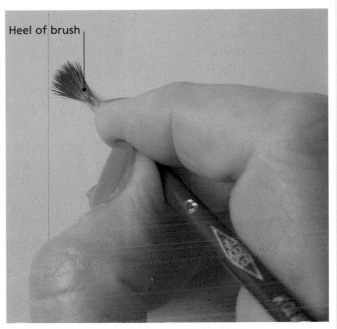

Heel of brush

2 Apply pressure on the toe to splay the hairs.

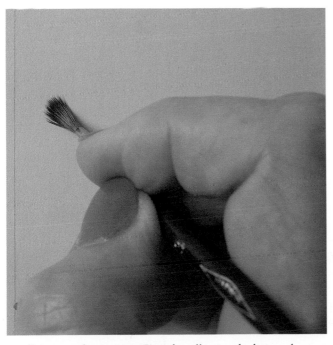

3 Bring your fingers into your palm, allowing the hairs to bounce back—the brush will pull away from the surface.

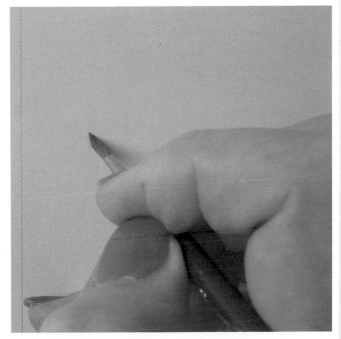

4 At the finishing position, the brush will have bounced back into its original shape.

Brushstrokes Step by Step

The following instructions should be referred to often until you become proficient in creating the thirteen basic brushstrokes. Once acquainted with these, you will then learn how to load the brush (i.e., double, triple and multiple loading). Do not rush the strokes. Move progressively through each, moving on to the next only once you have mastered the one before.

Brushstroke One

If you are left-handed, skip to brushstroke two. Hold your brush like a pen, with slightly outstretched fingers.

1 Start on the left side of the parallel lines. Apply pressure to the toe of the brush, causing the hairs to spread apart, and widening the stroke.

2 Simultaneously proceed to pull your fingers back into your palm from left to right. *Do not roll the brush.*

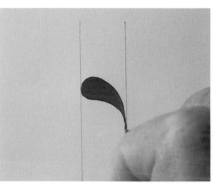

3 Guide the tail of the stroke toward the bottom of the page.

Brushstroke Two

Flick your wrist to the opposite side and adjust the paper, making sure that the brush lies at a 45° angle from right to left. By pulling the toe in the direction of the heel, the stroke will be fully filled out. Follow through slowly, examining each action.

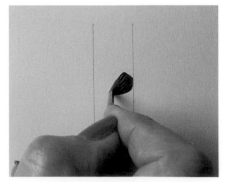

1 Start on the right side of the parallel lines. Apply pressure to the toe of the brush, causing the hairs to spread apart.

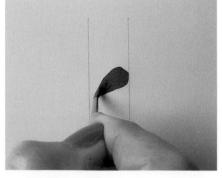

2 Simultaneously proceed to pull your fingers back into your palm from right to left. *Do not roll the brush.*

3 Guide the tail of the stroke toward the bottom of the page.

Painting Folk Art Flowers With Enid Hoessinger

Brushstroke Three

This "roll-pull" action is required for brushstrokes three, eight, nine and ten. The rolling action can be to the left or the right, depending on your grip at the time.

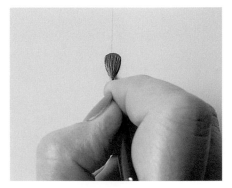 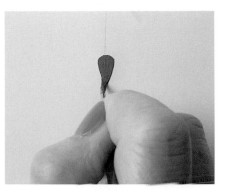 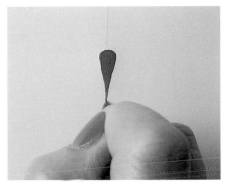

1 Direct the brush to lay parallel to the side of the page. Apply enough pressure on the toe to reach the required width.

2 Simultaneously lift, roll (a quarter-roll only) and pull your fingers into your palm. This lifting action will taper the stroke; the quarter-roll will bring the brush to a knife-edge, yielding a slender tail.

3 Guide the tail of the stroke toward the bottom of the page.

Brushstroke Four

Although the "stop-start, down-lift" action of this brushstroke appears very jerky, with practice it will flow smoothly. This brushstroke can stand by itself, but is chiefly designed to create the upper part of a rose leaf, with the second part being brushstroke six.

1 Start at the left side of the parallel line at a 45° angle. Barely touch the surface to draw a thin line toward the center. Stop!

2 Keeping the brush stationary, apply pressure to the toe.

3 Release pressure gradually while lifting the brush abruptly.

4 Complete the stroke with a very thin tail on the right side of the parallel line.

Brushstroke Five

This is the same as brushstroke four, but worked from right to left. It's designed to create the upper part of a rose leaf, with brushstroke seven as the lower half.

1 Start at the right side of the parallel line. Barely touch the surface to draw a thin line toward the center. Stop!

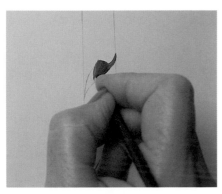

2 Keeping the brush stationary, apply pressure to the toe.

3 Release pressure gradually while lifting the brush abruptly.

4 Complete the stroke with a very thin tail on the left side of the parallel line.

Brushstroke Six

This stroke is designed as a follow-up stroke for brushstroke four. The movement should be fluid. This brushstroke starts on top of brushstroke four and melts, or links, together with it to create one point instead of two separate points.

1 Starting at the left side of the parallel line, barely touch the surface to draw a thin line steeply downward. Apply pressure *toward* the heel and stop. (Do not exert pressure *on* the heel.)

2 Immediately release the pressure from the heel, simultaneously dragging the toe *diagonally to the right* in a lifting manner.

3 At this point the brush has come to the tip at a knife-edge, and the tail (merely a token) is pulled downward.

Brushstroke Seven

This stroke is designed as a follow-up stroke for brushstroke five. It begins on top of brushstroke five and melts into it.

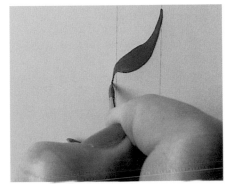

1 Starting at the right side of the parallel line, barely touch the surface to draw a thin line steeply downward. Apply pressure *toward* the heel and stop. (Do not exert pressure *on* the heel.)

2 Immediately release the pressure from the heel, simultaneously dragging the toe *diagonally to the left* in a lifting manner.

3 At this point the brush has come to the tip at a knife-edge, and the tail (merely a token) is pulled downward.

Brushstroke Eight

Brushstrokes eight, nine and ten can be used together as a set. Try to keep a flowing movement: Apply light pressure and lift in a gradual motion. The tapering at the base could be a little quicker to create a sudden narrowing. Roll to the left or right—whichever feels more comfortable.

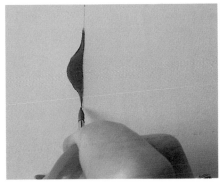

1 Hold the brush as for brushstroke three. Barely touch the surface. While pulling a short line, gradually push down and out toward the left.

2 Gradually lift and simultaneously roll-pull the brush, tapering the stroke.

3 Guide the tail toward the bottom of the page.

Brushstroke Nine

Roll to left or right for the tail.

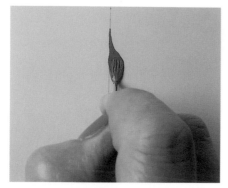 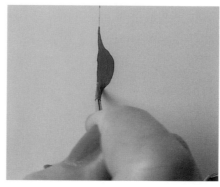 

1 Hold the brush as for brushstroke three. Barely touch the surface. While pulling a short line, gradually push the brush out toward the right.

2 Gradually lift and simultaneously roll-pull the brush, tapering the stroke.

3 Guide the tail toward the bottom of the page.

Brushstroke Ten

Roll to the left or right for the tail.

  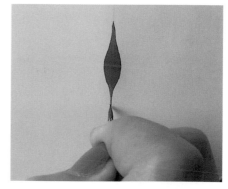

1 Hold the brush as for brushstroke three. Barely touch the surface. While pulling a short line, gradually push the brush against the surface—this will allow the hairs to splay out to both sides.

2 Gradually lift and simultaneously roll-pull the brush, tapering the stroke.

3 Guide the tail toward the bottom of the page.

Painting Folk Art Flowers With Enid Hoessinger

Brushstrokes Eleven and Twelve

These strokes, commonly referred to as *C-strokes*, are interlocked for a *Tölzer* rose (this style of folk rose, shown on page 12, originated in Bad Tölz in southern Bavaria) or can be used separately for C-stroke roses. I will use these strokes to teach brush application and color control.

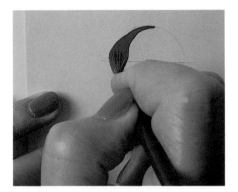

1 Hold the brush almost perpendicular to the surface, leaning slightly toward you. Start the stroke at the twelve o'clock position of the circle with a light touch, gradually adding pressure to the left.

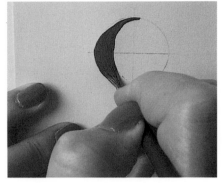

2 Retain maximum pressure at the girth of the stroke by *holding the brush down* while continuing with the stroke, swinging inward. The stroke is three-quarters done.

3 Slowly release the pressure and conclude the stroke, allowing the movement of your hand to follow through as though painting a circle. This will give roundness to the stroke.

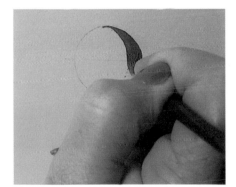

1 Hold the brush almost perpendicular to the surface, leaning slightly toward your body. Start in the same position as for brushstroke eleven, with a light touch, gradually adding pressure to the right.

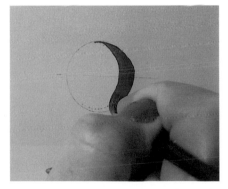

2 Retain maximum pressure at the girth of the stroke by *holding the brush down* while continuing with the stroke, swinging inward. The stroke is three-quarters done.

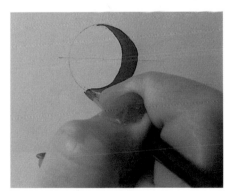

3 Slowly release the pressure and conclude the stroke, allowing the movement of your hand to follow through as though painting a circle. This will give roundness to the stroke.

Brushstroke Thirteen

This stroke forms scallops on a straight line, left to right. (Left-handed painters should work from right to left.)

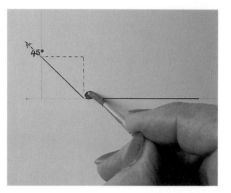

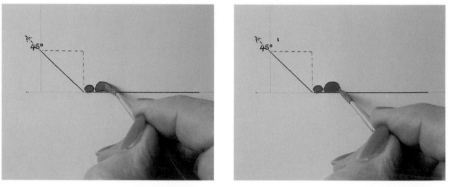

1 Hold the brush at a 45° angle at all times. Start at the left and work to the right. Touch the surface with the toe and lift. This will yield a dot.

2 Lift the brush toward the right. Do it again with a little more pressure on the toe. Lift the brush and repeat to the right, with a little more pressure every time, allowing a little space between.

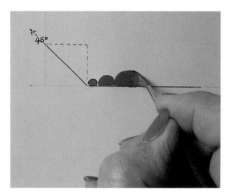

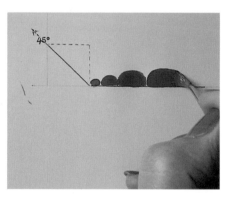

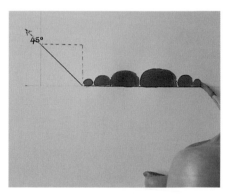

3 Check the brush—it should still lie at a 45° angle. Push the brush down on the toe (take note of the heel, which will remain on the line), hold it down, move to the right and then gradually lift. The toe will end where the heel used to be.

4 For larger scallops, hold the brush down while moving along to the required length; reduce the pressure for smaller scallops.

5 It's possible that the brush position will move out of the 45° angle, so move your hand along to keep the brush at the correct angle.

Painting Folk Art Flowers With Enid Hoessinger

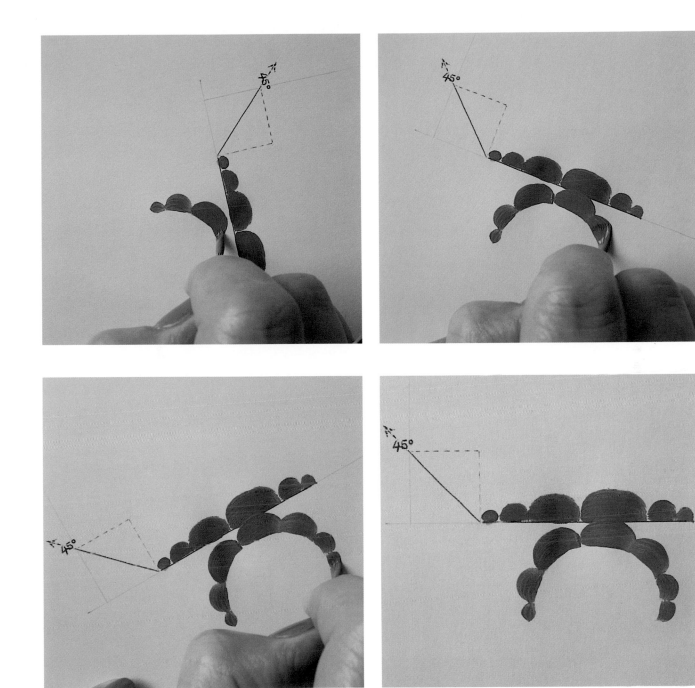

Now practice the same technique around a circle. Take note of the position of the paper: I've turned it upside down, working away from my hand in the same way as described previously. Paint approximately three petals, and then turn the paper again. Remember to start off small, increase and then decrease the scallop sizes, which will represent the petals toward the back of a rose. The scallops may be separated, or may be attached for double and triple petals. Definition between each scallop is created by moving on between scallops, holding the brush at a 45° angle at all times. These scallops form the outer petals for many different flowers at various levels.

Fixing Problems

Refer to the explanation of brush-strokes on pages 14–21 to correct these problems. These explanations will be of great assistance to you in the absence of a teacher. Try hard to master these strokes—they will be of infinite value as you unlock the secrets of the magical multi-loading technique.

Brushstrokes One and Two

   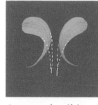  

A pointy start indicates the brush was moved on before pressure was applied. This is not a good brush-stroke one, but may work in a different application. Pressure to the toe before moving on will yield a round start.

The flat head indicates excessive pressure and waiting too long before moving on.

The angle of the brush was horizontal instead of at a 45° angle.

A curved tail is a bad habit, and doesn't allow the stroke—which represents a leaf—to attach naturally to a stem.

The heel of the brush shows—a result of a too-sudden lift. Do not help the brush.

The brushstroke does not taper after lifting—evidence of the brush being rolled in the fingers. Do not help the brush; tuck your fingers into your palm tightly.

Brushstrokes Three, Four and Five

   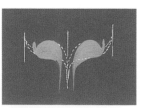 

A pointy start to the stroke results when the brush moves on before the pressure is down, making it more like a brush-stroke ten. Pressure to the toe before moving on will yield a round start.

A feathered tail is caused by not rolling the brush for completion. Only brushstrokes three, eight, nine and ten require the rolling action.

The body has been dragged too long and should taper quicker.

You've led the stroke, causing a crouched position. Do not help the brush.

After pressure was applied toward the heel, the toe was dragged downward, creating an S-stroke. The objective is to create the bulge to the base; therefore, the toe should be dragged across, not down. An S-stroke is fine, but cannot be attached to brushstroke four or five for a rose leaf.

Brushstrokes Eleven and Twelve

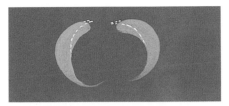 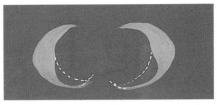 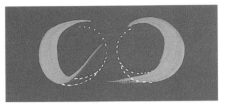

Don't start with pressure. All the paint will be used where it's not needed, and will run out where it counts most. Start lightly, pressure and lift.

Pressure was lifted off too soon, creating a stroke that is inadequate in width. Hold the pressure down three-quarters of the way, and then lift gradually.

This is typical of a fast flick at the end. When completing the stroke, be careful not to flick the brush in haste; instead, follow through as if completing a circle in midair.

Brushstroke Thirteen

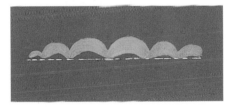

These scallops are not filled out to the line, indicating you were drawing with the brush. Do not help the brush. Merely apply pressure to the toe, ensuring that the brush lies at a 45° angle.

The entire brush was pushed down to the heel instead of applying pressure on the toe only. Therefore the whole footprint of the brush is visible. A similar effect is achieved when the brush is no longer at a 45° angle.

All scallops are butting against each other. Move on between each scallop to make room for the next.

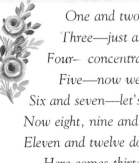

These scallops are weak, indicating that the brush is no longer at a 45° angle, but is parallel to the line. Try again.

One and two are easy to do.
Three—just as easy you'll see.
Four— concentrate a little bit more.
Five—now we're coming alive.
Six and seven—let's send them to heaven.
Now eight, nine and ten give us hope again.
Eleven and twelve don't belong on the shelf.
Here comes thirteen, lucky for some;
Keep it working, for there's lots more fun.

Chapter Four

Loading Your Brush and Painting Foliage

As you work through this chapter, take time to carefully read *every* instruction, and look at the brush frequently so that you can familiarize yourself with the results. Work your way, in order, from the beginning through to the end. Rather than just teaching you the individual terms and brush loading techniques, I've used the techniques to demonstrate how to paint foliage. Multi-loading techniques are demonstrated on a basic rose.

Do not wash your brush until instructions tell you to do so. This is particularly important to know from the start. Also, be sure that the viscosity of the white has been reduced. Have a palette, a paper towel, a jar of water and some paper ready. Moisten the brush in water, and pull the brush over the paper towel to remove any excess water.

Loading

Loading means preparing your brush with one color—this is referred to as a *single load*. When loading the brush, all of the hairs need to be filled with paint—not just the tip or the visible outside, but inside the hairs of the brush right up to the metal ferrule.

Make sure you've added water to your white paint, as directed on page 10.

1 Holding the brush at a 45° angle, tap the bristles into the paint (in this case, a dark green made by mixing 4 parts Antique Green to 1 part Lamp Black) while rolling the handle between your fingers. This fills the brush; the excess must be rolled off before you begin painting. You will also need Yellow Light and Titanium White on your palette, placed approximately two finger spaces apart.

Fill It Up

The brushes we are using are made of natural sable hair, allowing us to fill the brush to the metal ferrule—unlike its synthetic counterpart, where you are correctly advised not to.

Expelling the Excess

Moving the brush with a roll-pull action next to the puddle reduces the amount of paint in the brush while smoothing the hair. This is known as *dressing the brush*—think of it as getting the brush ready for the next step. Just how much paint to expel depends on the size of the strokes required.

If a large stroke is to be painted in just one color, leave enough paint on the brush to paint approximately ten strokes, large to small. Practice this, and take note of the amount of paint you must leave in the brush to get ten strokes—this will give you a feel for the quantity required. Never paint with a bloated brush, which will only create unwanted texture. Keep your palette tidy.

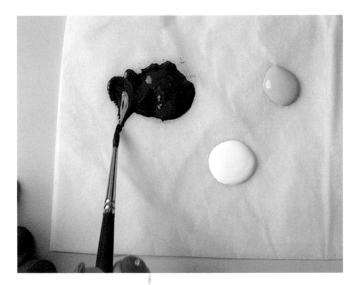

2 With paint in the brush, roll and pull it into your hand at approximately a 30° angle over the palette.

3 Repeat this action several times, depending on the size of the stroke you'll be painting. The length of space required next to your paint puddle is approximately three times the length of the brush hairs.

Loading Your No. 5 Sable Brush

This brush can easily be overloaded, so take special care when loading. Moisten the brush with water and dry it over a paper towel. Do not plunge the brush into a big puddle of paint; instead, lift some paint away from the puddle and push the paint into the brush in a tapping, rolling manner. Look at the brush. The hairs should be visible through the paint.

Lifting

A lift, as the word suggests, is an upward motion. Lifting is used to add another color to the brush. The paint is taken away from the puddle in order to proceed. The brush is still not ready after lifting, because the second color merely sits on top. We are looking for gradation of color, so we will sweep the brush (as explained in step 6).

Sweeping

Sweeping refers to pulling or wiping the brush over the surface of the palette, completing a double or triple load. This action is very specific: When sweeping a floor we apply pressure to remove the dirt; so, too, we "sweep" the brush over the surface of the palette. Holding the second color face-down, sweep once, twice or as many times as necessary. Every time the brush is swept over the surface, the lifted color will be pushed into the brush and the excess paint will be removed, preventing an overloaded brush. Sweeping a second color blends the two colors within the brush. A short, gentle sweep is used when only the toe of the brush has lifted color.

There is a limit to the amount of sweeping you should do—do not mute the colors. Although I will instruct you to the approximate number of sweeps needed for strokes in this book, practice will provide the answers to your specific needs.

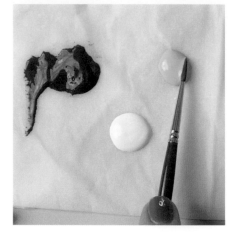

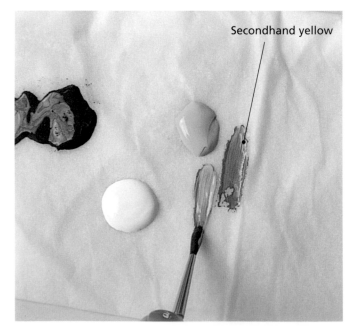

Secondhand yellow

Incorrect Lifting

By scooping instead of lifting, the second color will wrap around the tip of the brush, distorting the double load. Another common mistake is lifting the second color on the tip only, instead of on the entire side of the brush.

4 Touch the side of the brush "dressed" with dark green into a second color (Yellow Light here), just far enough to cover one side with the second color.

5 To complete the "lift," pull your fingers into your palm as previously described. This will pull the second color toward the tip of the brush, preventing a blob of paint hanging off the side.

6 Hold the "lifted" yellow to face the surface of the palette. Pull the brush along in a sweeping motion, about twice the length of the sable. Do this three or four times to lighten the green in the brush.

7 Lift fresh yellow and sweep on a clean spot once. On the inside of the brush, the two colors are working hard at making a subtle gradation.

Single-Loading

Single-loading refers to only one color in the brush (see *loading*, step one).

Double-Loading

Double-loading refers to having two colors on the brush, as demonstrated in steps four through seven. When you load a second color, make sure you have expelled the excess so that you do not bloat the brush. The colors can be swept repeatedly in order to achieve gradation; (see *lifting* and *sweeping*).

Triple-Loading

Triple-loading is a method of layered sweeping. Three colors can be layered in the same way as double-loading. Generally Antique Gold Deep or Yellow Light is used as a buffer between two colors, hence the triple load.

Before trying the following exercise on your own, read the instructions through to page 28. Then double-load dark green plus Yellow Light as instructed on the previous pages and follow steps 8 and 9 to achieve a triple load. Now try the triple-load exercise. Look at the dark side of your brush and note how the volume of paint has pushed through to the opposite side.

8 In previous steps, we loaded dark green in the brush, removed the excess paint and then lifted Yellow Light and swept it. Now add the third color by lifting Titanium White on the Yellow Light side.

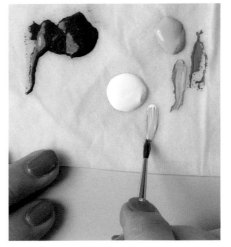

9 Sweep once firmly on a clean spot.

Triple-Load Exercise

With a triple load in the brush, hold the dark green to the right and the white to the left (side-load application) and paint a good-size brushstroke ten (see page 18). Notice how the lifting technique has protected the dark green from meeting the white on the brush by buffering it with yellow, resulting in a subtle change from dark to light green. The most important thing here is that the dark green and white on the same brush did not turn gray.

If your brushstroke *has* turned gray, you may have started either with too little yellow or too much dark green in your brush. If your brushstroke is too light, you have added too much white.

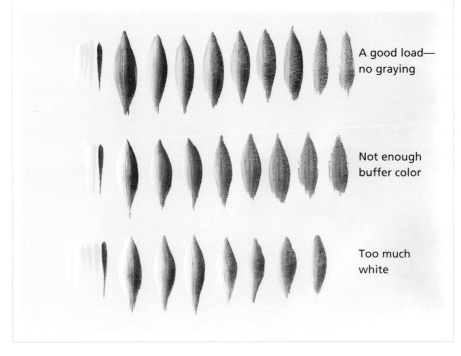

A good load—no graying

Not enough buffer color

Too much white

Reloading the Brush

1. When a reload is required in the same colors, the dark side of the brush is swept through a little paint that has been "pulled out" from the darkest color. Replace the yellow by holding the white side down and sweeping firmly through the pulled-out yellow paint once or twice (you do not need to remove the white). Replace the white by sweeping through the "secondhand" (pulled-out) white area on your palette. Continue to reload the brush in this manner for the duration of foliage painting, without washing the brush. When the yellow area next to your puddle is used up, more can be lifted and then swept in the same spot. When the secondhand white is used up, lift a little fresh white, and again sweep through the white once in the same spot.

2. When a darker stroke is required, sweep through yellow once on the dark side and then through dark green once on the same side.

3. When a lighter stroke is required, sweep through the yellow once or twice on the light side and then replace the white as mentioned previously.

Applying What You've Learned

Are you mind-boggled? Well, if you are, it is time to get those paints out and try the exercise on page 27. If it doesn't work the first time, do not despair—just try it again. Pay attention to the way you hold the brush. Never roll it around in your fingers; do be constantly aware of where the light and dark sides are.

Here's another chance to test your skills. To paint foliage, we mainly use brushstrokes one to ten. Try painting brushstrokes eight and nine with the light to the outside—this will form a rose leaf. If the color was not swept in well enough, you will have a sudden light edge. Try to achieve good gradation.

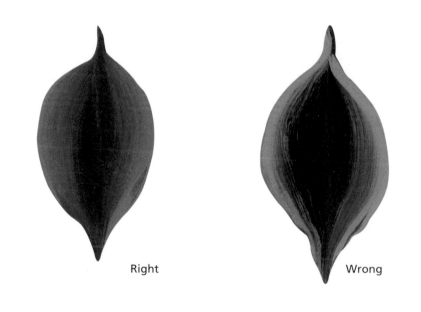

Right   Wrong

What Am I Doing Wrong?

Problem: The sweeping area has accumulated murky color.
Solution: You are reloading when there is still sufficient color in the brush.

Problem: I could not get a neat brushstroke.
Solution: Flatten the brush over a clean spot once on the dark side (this action will pull the balance of dark down to the tip again) and then once through a little yellow and once through a little secondhand white.

Problem: My color is too light.
Solution: Darken the dark side.

Problem: My color is too dark.
Solution: Lighten the light side using both yellow and white.

Tapping

Tapping is similar to the sweeping process, without the pulling action. The purpose is to connect, not blend, the newly lifted color with the colors in the brush.

Strike-Backs

This is a very specific stroke—not unlike a sweep—that yields some interesting effects. A strike-back is always done with the dark side of the brush facing down and applied with the light side held mostly to the surface. It can be done through a little paint or over a clean palette. The latter will not add paint to the brush; the former will replace the paint used and will gradually darken the subject. This technique is used to achieve special effects. The instructions will guide you in when and how to use it.

Washes

Washes are used mainly on light-colored backgrounds when the dark foliage color provides too much contrast. Thin your darkest foliage color with water to make it like ink, and then paint between the foliage areas to create the depth and solidity needed in some designs. In some cases, you may need to reduce (or increase) the amount of color to adjust the intensity. Never overfill the brush, because this will cause puddles that, when dry, become blotches instead of delicate, distant foliage.

Washes can be painted before, during or after the design is painted. For best results, paint larger, underlying washes before the flowers are laid in place.

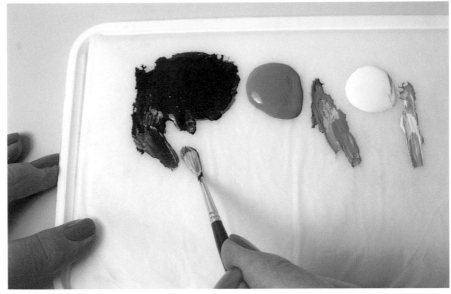

With your brush triple-loaded and white the last color swept, turn the brush over, dark side down, and strike back with one sweep over the palette. The result of this action will be a darker effect.

To make a wash, take a little dark-green foliage color and thin it with water.

Preparing the Foliage

Steps one through fifteen below use techniques you've already learned to paint foliage for a multi-loaded rose. The multi-loading demonstration begins with step sixteen.

1 With the main foliage color in the brush, I have started with brushstroke five, pulling the stroke over the rose tracing to close all gaps between the rose and the foliage.

2 Brushstroke seven attaches to brushstroke five.

3 Brushstrokes four and six on opposite sides will create a gap.

4 The gap is closed with an S-stroke. Do not draw the brush.

5 Lift the Antique Gold Deep on one side of the brush.

6 Sweep the brush over the palette next to the Antique Gold Deep puddle (creating a secondhand gold) for medium foliage.

7 Paint the overlapping leaves with Antique Gold Deep toward the previously painted dark leaf. Complete all medium foliage.

8 Sweep the gold side of the brush through gold again, and then lift Titanium White on the gold side.

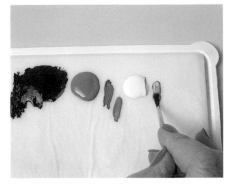  

9 With white face down, sweep only *once* over the palette next to the white puddle (this will create a secondhand white).

10 Hold the white toward the right in preparation for the following strokes.

11 Repeat brushstroke two, slightly smaller, with white still to the right.

12 Repeat loading by sweeping the light side through secondhand Antique Gold Deep, and then sweep through secondhand white, holding the white to the left.

13 The turn-back is done in the same manner, with white to the right.

14 Refer to page 37 to create a knife-edge. Paint the center vein on the leaf with the brush upright.

15 Here the veining has been completed and the underlying foliage has been washed in (see page 29 for washes).

Multi-Loading

For this technique color mixing (layering more than three colors from the palette) is required. Specific colors with strong pigment are necessary for successful results; frequently, I will instruct you to use only a little white.

The following demonstration is a triple load using the multi-load technique for an easy start. For now, don't worry too much about how the rose is formed: This will be taught in chapter six. Instead, concentrate on how the brush is multi-loaded and the effects it creates when it is applied.

16 Mix equal parts Antique Green and Brilliant Red to form the base color for this flower. Mix the color with your brush by pulling the colors together in strokelike manner. Don't scrub the hairs of the brush. When the brush is properly loaded, expel the excess color to make space for additional colors. Lift Antique Gold Deep.

17 Sweep twice next to the paint puddle.

18 Lift white on the gold side.

19 Sweep over the white side once on a clean spot. The paint left behind is your secondhand white.

20 With the white to the top, paint three small, irregular brushstroke thirteens.

21 With the light side in the same position, paint two large brushstroke thirteens.

22 Lift white and paint the left side of the rose. (See page 49.)

23 Lift white and paint the right side of rose in the same manner.

24 Lift white again, and paint a scallop for the front petal. (See page 49, step 3.)

25 Replace white; paint brushstroke three in the center.

26 Complete the right side of the front petal with brushstroke ones.

Painting Folk Art Flowers With Enid Hoessinger

27 Replace the white and repeat this process for the opposite side with brushstroke twos.

28 Darken the dark side as follows: Sweep the dark side through secondhand gold, and then sweep the same side through the dark base color.

29 Paint the side petals. (See page 50, step 4.)

30 Increase the white for the light outer petals.

31 Continue the outer petals.

32 Increase the white and paint the final front petal.

Painting Folk Art Flowers With Enid Hoessinger

Preparing a Knife-Edge

1 Load in the usual manner, rolling off excess paint. Sweep firmly over the palette; the brush will remain flattened. Turn the brush over and repeat this sweeping action on the same spot on the palette.

2 Observe how flat the brush appears when viewed from the side. This is called a *knife-edge single load*.

Double-Loading a Knife-Edge

1 Complete steps 1 and 2 for a single load, and then lift Antique Gold Deep on one flat side of the brush. Holding the gold to face the surface of the palette, sweep firmly over the palette once or twice.

2 When the brush is turned over, observe how much gold still remains after one sweep.

Tips for Painting With a Knife-Edge

- To reload a knife-edge brush, sweep once firmly on the dark side and then once on the light side. Remember that the last color on the brush will be the first color off (or the dominant color in the stroke).
- For lighter strokes, sweep through the light color last.
- For darker strokes, sweep through the dark color last.
- To reload all colors, repeat the instructions for loading, ending with the color required for the next stroke.
- To yield very fine strokes, often sweeping on the same spot of the appropriate color on the palette will be sufficient for a reload. This will prevent the brush from becoming overloaded.

Triple-Loading
a Knife-Edge

1 Double-load the brush as instructed on the previous page, and then lift a little Titanium White on the gold side of the brush. Sweep once with the white facing down.

2 Here the brush has been turned over to show the white already swept into it.

3 Seen from the side, the brush is still formed to a knife-edge, with one dark side and one light side.

Painting
Knife-Edge Strokes

1 Apply a little pressure for brushstroke three, holding the brush perpendicular to the surface.

2 Continue to tuck your fingers further into your palm until the brush leaves the surface.

3 For darker strokes, sweep the dark over the palette once and then observe the dark side of the brush.

Single load
These strokes are often used as filler strokes between leaves to represent finer foliage. Watered-down green is used to represent more distant foliage.

Double load
The double-loaded stroke will be lighter than the single load.

Triple load
The stroke is widest at the start and will get narrower as the brush gradually pulls away from the surface. Paint many of these short, jerky strokes to vein leaves.

A leaf veined with knife-edge strokes.

Brush Application for Color Control

There are three ways to apply the loaded brush, with minor variations. (These variations will be explained in the instructions.)

1. With the light color directed either to the left or the right, so that all the colors on the brush are visible (side-load application)

2. With the light color facing down to the surface

3. With the light color facing up to the ceiling

Color Control in Brushstroke Thirteen

When practicing on a straight line, white should face the top of the page, or away from oneself, for both the right- and left-handed.

Side-loading applied to left and right

Light side down to the surface

Light side up to the ceiling

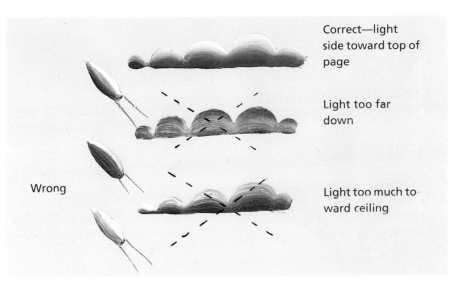

Correct—light side toward top of page

Light too far down

Wrong

Light too much toward ceiling

Which Side of the Brush Do I Use?

Try not to be confused by the "sides" of the brush, as we are dealing with a round brush. When you apply pressure to the brush, it will alter its form, creating a flat side. This flat side can be alternated by the way you apply the brush. Because the brush is round, any side can be applied; however, when you load a second color this immediately stipulates a side and commits the brush to a light and a dark side. While we are loading, it seems as if we flatten the brush—this is obvious when you look at a loaded brush from the side. When you apply the brush so both colors are visible, the brush will flatten that edge as well.

A Recap of Foliage Procedure

If you've followed along in order with the various brush-loading techniques in this chapter, you've also been learning to paint foliage. Use these instructions when painting any foliage throughout the book.

1. Paint the washes, if necessary.
2. Block out the darkest foliage in a single load.
3. Paint medium foliage in a double load.
4. Paint lightest foliage in a triple load.
5. Refer to chapter nine for layout guidelines indicating separation of foliage.

Chapter Five

Combination Brushstrokes

The objective of the painting alphabet is to create form with minimal brushstrokes. Once this technique is mastered, it will be easy for you to read a pattern and easier still for you to recognize the approach necessary to paint any flower. After acquainting yourself with these strokes, you will see commas everywhere you look. This chapter will help you recognize the use of each stroke and how the strokes can be combined to create different shapes. It's important to be well-practiced in the strokes before starting to combine them. Needless to say, brush loading is important and will give you a wonderful insight into the process.

Note the direction each flower takes—simple yet effective.

Brushstrokes one, two and three make sense when used together, creating movement within flowers.

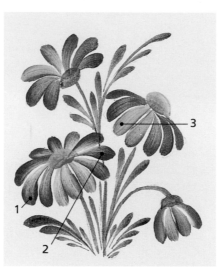

Daisy made with full brushstroke three

Daisy made with flattened, knife-edge brushstroke three

Daisy made with shortened brushstroke three–leave off tails

Brushstroke three works well for a repeated design. A knife-edge daisy makes a good filler flower; observe the rigid look in the absence of brushstrokes one and two. These brushstrokes can be stretched, shortened, fattened or thinned.

Combined for leaves

Brushstrokes four and six, and brushstrokes five and seven, are specifically designed to form rose leaves.

Combined for leaves

Brushstrokes four and six—with tails cut off—form the left rose petal. Brushstrokes five and seven—with tails cut off—form the right rose petal.

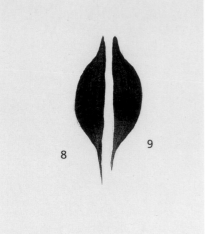

Combined to form a rose leaf

Brushstrokes eight and nine are combined for rose leaves, but can also be used for different elements. Note how easy it is to get the light side to work magic, using the same strokes.

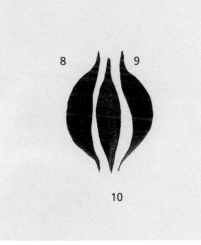

Quick large leaves

Brushstrokes eight, nine and ten are capable of painting large elements quickly. Combine these strokes to paint larger concave petals on a daisy, with the light side to the outside. A tulip is painted in the opposite manner, holding the light side to the center to create a convex shape.

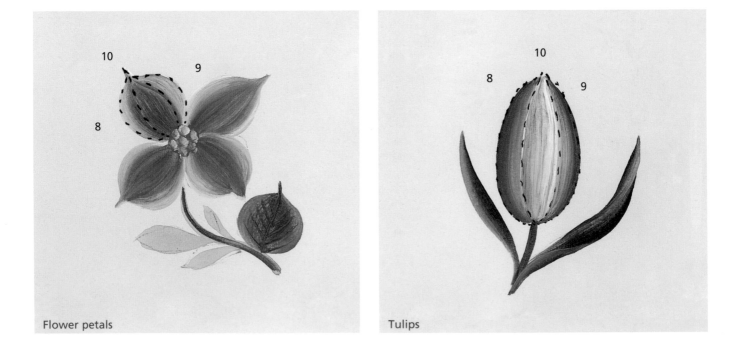

Flower petals

Tulips

Painting Folk Art Flowers With Enid Hoessinger

Keep white to the inside

11

Brushstroke eleven doubled up

Keep white
to the inside

12

Brushstroke twelve doubled up

Brushstroke eleven can be used on its own—singly or doubled up—to form the bowl of a rose. Brushstroke twelve can also be used on its own in the same manner. The white will be most intense at the beginning of these strokes, creating a light source. Choose which stroke to use according to your light source.

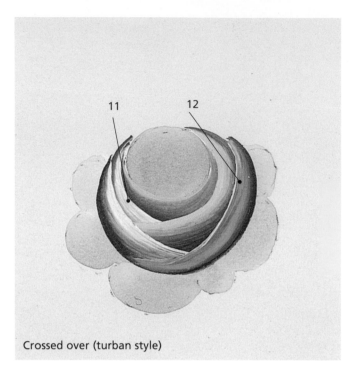

Crossed over (turban style)

These combined brushstrokes eleven and twelve are overlapped alternately to indicate petal formation.

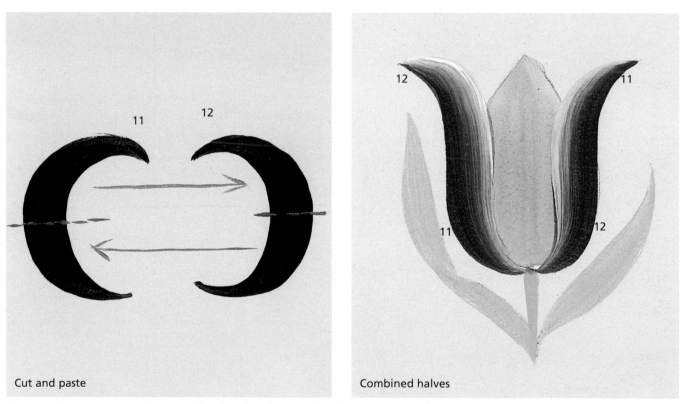

Cut and paste

Combined halves

Cutting and pasting tops and bottoms of brushstrokes eleven and twelve and swapping them can be used to form a tulip and its leaves.

Painting Folk Art Flowers With Enid Hoessinger

The following strokes will create new effects without adding brushstrokes to our painting alphabet.

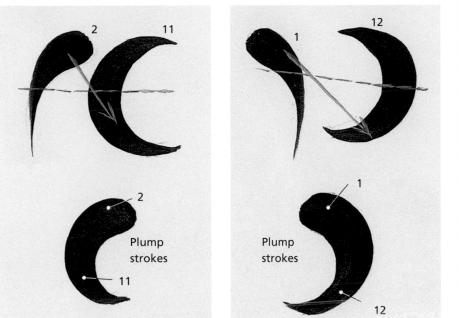

Brushstroke three closes the gap

2nd   3rd   1st

The 1-2-3 stroke—overlap and close the gap

Brushstrokes two and eleven, and brushstrokes one and twelve, can be used in a cut-and-paste manner to achieve plump strokes. The objective is to create speedy and accurate circles as filler. I call this the *1-2-3 stroke* because it is that easy.

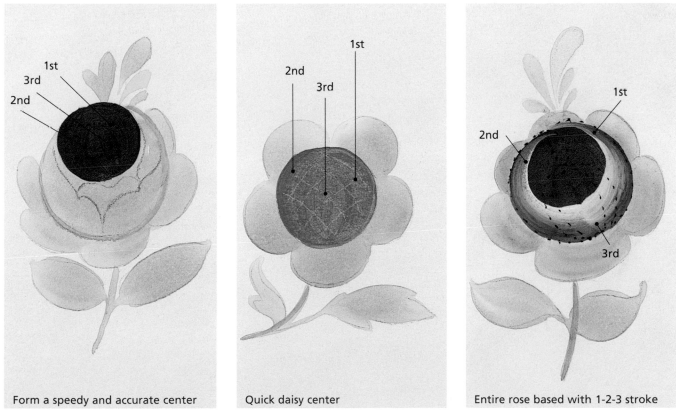

Form a speedy and accurate center

Quick daisy center

Entire rose based with 1-2-3 stroke

This circle could be the center of a rose or a daisy, or the entire base of a rose (using combination strokes to embellish it).

Brushstroke thirteen is one of the most used brushstrokes, so it is well worth getting the hang of it. It can be used multiple times per flower. The stroke is versatile small or large, and will give unlimited results. Use it by itself in varying sizes to create distance around the rose. The strokes can be doubled up or even tripled.

Brushstroke thirteen in various sizes

Brushstroke thirteen wrapped around a rose

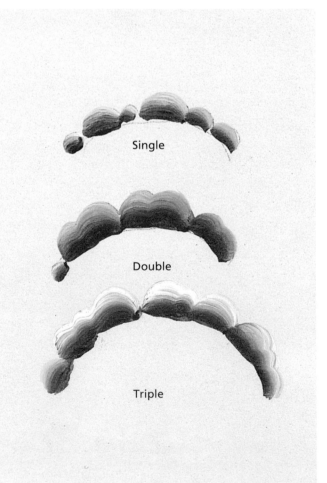

Single

Double

Triple

Painting Folk Art Flowers With Enid Hoessinger

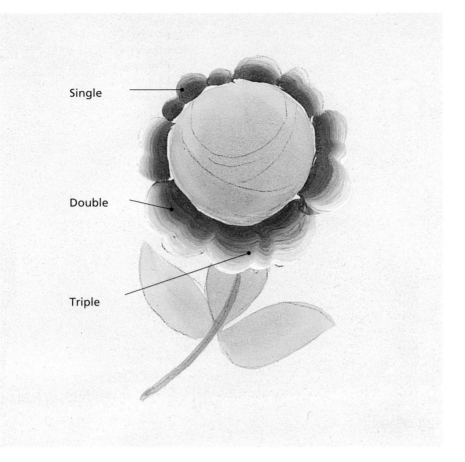

Single

Double

Triple

13

1

2

These petals are started using light deposits of white made with small brushstroke thirteens. The individual scallops are not necessarily attached. Brushstrokes one, two and three are used to complete the petal.

Brushstroke thirteen starts each petal

Chapter Six

Painting a Rose

This chapter will help you understand the formation of roses while teaching you how to make colors gradate from dark to light. Once you have grasped this method, you will be able to paint any variation you choose. Each rose design is laid out differently and becomes a guide for you to work from.

The projects provide examples of how to combine the various segments of a rose and an outline to form petals, centers and skirts. Select a rose you want to paint—there are three variations—and then follow the steps on these pages for that type. Throughout this book you will find other variations of these roses. The basic principles described here remain the same. The most important thing to remember is that the side petals should be darker than the front petals to create the appearance of depth. Use white to lighten, rather than outline, the design. Do not hurry—take one step at a time. Making mistakes is the only way to learn.

Don't "outline" with white

Pull the white into the stroke to lighten

Variation One

1. Painting the Mouth of the Rose

This center has great depth and is used for elementary or intermediate roses. It is the same in all three variations. Use brushstroke thirteen and a no. 3 or a no. 4 brush.

Paint a single brushstroke thirteen, triple-loaded. The dark side is now in the "throat" of the rose.

Immediately above and overlapping the first stroke, paint another thirteen, exaggerating its size with a slight drawing action.

Above and overlapping the second stroke, paint another thirteen, again increasing the size.

Work from the bottom up.

Overlap the strokes so the dark on the brush blends with the previous deposit of dark in the stroke, thus leaving the dark behind in every stroke and creating depth. Your last stroke will contain the least amount of dark.

Follow the top of the curve with small, irregular brushstroke thirteens.

Paint two thin brushstroke ones at the base of these.

2. Forming a Rose Bowl

In this variation, the bowl has two sides that are joined by a central front petal.

Start by increasing the white on your brush and doing a short strike-back. Lightly paint a hook on the left with white held to one o'clock.

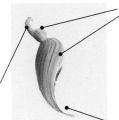

Immediately apply a little pressure for two small thirteens; lift sharply between them.

As if changing your mind, complete a brushstroke two with a tucked-in tail. The white should be left behind.

Follow up with brushstroke eleven on the outside. This should be worked from the back.

Work forward, repeating brushstroke two to meet the white.

Each stroke overlaps the previous one.

Side petals are assembled like this.

Again replace the white on your brush, do a short strike-back, and then paint a hook on the right and brushstroke one all in one action, with a tucked-in tail. Follow up with brushstroke twelve on the outside, completing this petal.

3. Painting the Front Petal

Reload white as before. Paint three brushstroke thirteens in an up-down-up manner to create a curve or dip.

Hold white to the surface and paint brushstroke three in the center.

Paint several brushstroke twos on the left, with the white held to the surface.

Fractionally turn the brush toward the dark side for each stroke. This will result in gradual darkening for outer sides. Do not clean the brush.

Paint several brushstroke ones on the right, with the white held to the surface.

Again, fractionally turn the brush.

4. Painting the Outer Petals (Skirt)

Reload the brush with dark color and paint two brushstroke twos on the left. Overlap the bowl.

Sweep on the dark side again and paint one brushstroke one on the right, with the dark facing the rose.

Reload the brush by lifting and tapping the white for each of the two front petals; turn the rose upside down and push away from the rose in pressure-lift manner, using brush-stroke thirteen. You may wash the brush.

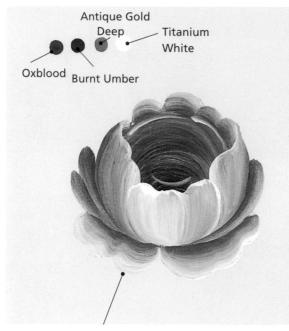

Take note of the white edges getting lost against the light background.

When supportive foliage is included, the white shows up well, creating an illusion of depth.

Tips for Painting a Rose

- Check the viscosity of your white and, if necessary, adjust it before starting.
- Do not roll the brush around without awareness of your light and dark sides.
- Do not wash the brush until the rose is fully painted.
- Do not add dark unless instructed to do so.

Variation Two

1. Painting the Mouth of the Rose

This step is the same as for variation one.

Paint a single brushstroke thirteen, triple-loaded. The dark side is now in the "throat" of the rose.

Immediately above and overlapping the first stroke, paint another thirteen, exaggerating its size with a slight drawing action.

Above and overlapping the second stroke, paint another thirteen, again increasing the size.

Work from the bottom up.

Overlap the strokes so the dark on the brush blends with the previous deposit of dark in the stroke, thus leaving the dark behind in every stroke and creating depth. Your last stroke will contain the least amount of dark.

Follow the top of the curve with small, irregular brushstroke thirteens. Paint two thin brushstroke ones at the base of these.

2. Forming a Rose Bowl

In this variation you will walk the strokes close together. There is no central front petal; instead, the two sides join or overlap.

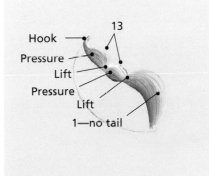

Replace the white on your brush and tap it gently. Paint a small hook, followed by two brushstroke thirteens and a brushstroke one. This should leave white behind.

Now start at the back, with the white still facing the front (leaving dark on the outer edge), and paint brushstroke eleven to link with the hook.

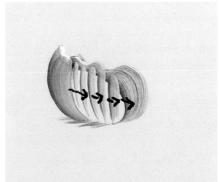

Lay brushstroke two tightly inside of eleven and follow up with 5 or more brushstroke twos in that small space; apply pressure, gathering white as you go. Move forward only a fraction at a time, slowly turning the white to face down in front. This is called *walking the brush* toward the white.

Gradation must be dark to light

Petals join

Light at the front

Do the same on the opposite side, ending brushstroke two or three with no tail. Paint brushstroke twelve at the back to link with the hook, followed by brushstroke one.

Note how every brushstroke is lower as the brush moves forward, joining the front stroke.

3. Painting the Outside Petals

This step is the same for every rose, whether you paint bowl variation one, two or three.

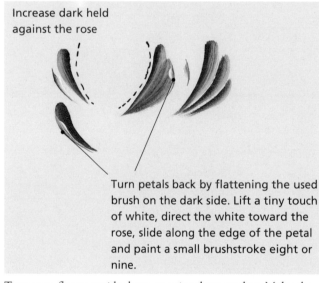

Increase dark held against the rose

Turn petals back by flattening the used brush on the dark side. Lift a tiny touch of white, direct the white toward the rose, slide along the edge of the petal and paint a small brushstroke eight or nine.

Turn your flower upside down to paint these strokes. Make the petals darker and narrower toward the back and lighter in front. From time to time, change the width of the strokes, applying pressure with the brush at a 45° angle. A deliberate attempt should be made to vary the petals from side to side. You don't want to end up with a rose that looks like it's wearing Mickey Mouse ears.

Turn-backs

Turn-backs are edges of petals or leaves that flip over the inner surface, revealing a portion of the outer surface. They can give character to plain outer petals, or lift the flower from a background where there is no foliage. Although turn-backs are nice, don't go overboard. More is not necessarily better. Justify each turn-back.

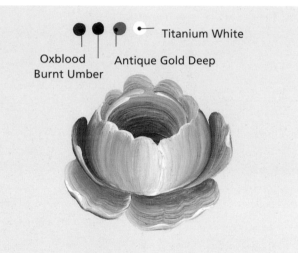

Oxblood
Burnt Umber

Antique Gold Deep

Titanium White

This gold-toned, variation two rose indicates justified turn-backs.

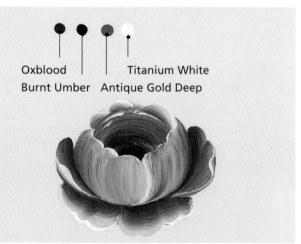

Oxblood
Burnt Umber

Antique Gold Deep

Titanium White

Here is the same rose done in a darker mauve color. Although I used the same colors for all three variations, subtle color changes can be made by increasing or decreasing the amount of Antique Gold Deep used. Altering the tone of roses within the same palette is characteristic of the multi-loading technique.

Painting Folk Art Flowers With Enid Hoessinger

Variation Three

Extra Petal

Paint the rose as for variation two, and then add the front petal from step 3 of variation one, creating a front petal that overlaps the joining side petals.

Petal Tip

When painting alternating petals, outer and inner petals should not correspond.

Variation three front petal

What Am I Doing Wrong?

Problem: I can't get the white to pull into the stroke.
Solution: Reduce the viscosity of the white.

Problem: My rose is too dark.
Solution: Start with less dark in the brush, or add less dark when replacing the paint in the brush during execution of the rose.

Problem: My rose is muddy.
Solution: Your white got into the dark side of the brush, or into the dark color on the palette.

Problem: I'm having trouble painting the skirt of the rose in one stroke.
Solution: Take heart, this requires practice. Turn the rose upside down in order to push away from the rose and into the light on the brush, and make sure that the brush lies at a 45° angle. If all else fails, wait for the skirt to dry and close the gaps.

Chapter Seven

Preparing Your Surface

Now that you've learned the basic techniques for painting folk art flowers, it's time to show off your new skills on a finished project. Flowers painted with the multi-loading technique will embellish any surface: wood, paper, cardboard, fabric, canvas, plastics, glass or metal. There are no limitations to what you can paint, be it a piece of furniture or a single button. Keep in mind that some of these surfaces may require other mediums—use the medium appropriate for the surface, such as fabric paint for fabric and glass paint for glass.

Use surfaces that appeal to you and that are proportionate in size. My choices of articles are purely topical suggestions. Use articles you would like to see in your home. Maybe something you already have in your attic will prove to be a perfect candidate to restore, giving it a new life and you a lot of pleasure.

Wood always provides a good finish and stands up well to wear and tear. Less expensive "craft wood" surfaces or particleboard pieces are ideal for large articles and fancy shapes. Seal these materials with sanding sealer before painting to prevent them from becoming "furry." Allow the sealer to dry well before sanding it back with steel wool, and then proceed as directed at right.

These are just a few of the wide varieties of surfaces available.

Preparing Wooden Surfaces

1. Your finished work can suffer as a result of shortcuts taken in preparation. Take each project one step at a time. If articles have imperfections, fill them with wood filler and allow them to dry thoroughly before sanding. When sanding, take particular care with profiled edges where the grain has been cross cut, as these may need a little more work. Fold the sandpaper in quarters for a firm edge to access corners.

Apply wood filler to imperfections with a palette knife. When thoroughly dry, sand smooth.

2. Complete the background of your project the night before, allowing plenty of time for drying. If you must do a last-minute basecoat, at least wait until the painted surface no longer feels cold before sanding it. Use a blow-dryer to ensure the surface is dry, but do not allow the piece to get hot.

3. When water is applied to wood, the grain lifts. Learn to use this to your advantage by moistening the area with a rag to open the grain. You are now ready for the first coat of paint. This step will not only make application much easier, but will also allow the paint to soak right into the wood, which is what I expect of a basecoat. Drying may take a little longer, but the finished surface is well worth the trouble.

4. Pour a little paint into a saucer and thin it slightly with water. Apply the paint with the brush of your choice in the direction of the wood grain. Use a household brush for a more textured effect or a flat brush for a smoother finish (the surface doesn't have to be devoid of tooth). Cover the entire article with the first coat of paint (edges to be painted in a complementing color are done last). Allow the project to dry thoroughly.

5. Sand lightly, with fine sandpaper, in the direction of the grain.

6. Apply a second coat of paint, slightly thicker than the first, with the wood grain. This coat will dry a lot faster than the previous one. If the surface is very rough, sand it again lightly. Always finish with a thin coat of paint, because the last coat of paint provides the tooth for the decoration to adhere to.

7. Follow the same steps to paint the back of the article. It's very important to seal the wood equally all over to prevent warping or twisting.

Basecoat the entire surface and allow it to dry.

Sand lightly in the direction of the grain.

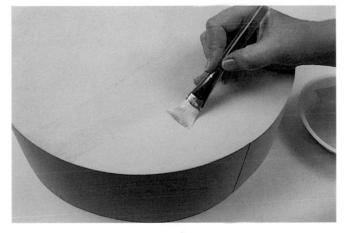

Apply a second, thicker coat. Sand again if needed, and apply a thin final coat.

Saving Paint and the Environment

In order to save paint and care for the environment, do not wash your brush between basecoats; instead, wrap it in plastic to keep the paint moist. After basecoating, save the leftover paint by cleaning the brush off on another article or sample board. When you change your rinse water, pour the old water into a bucket and allow it to stand overnight. The paint will settle to the bottom so you can pour the water off in the garden or down the drain, and then wipe out the paint residue with used paper towels.

Chapter Eight

Painting a Design

Now that you've chosen a surface and prepared it for painting, decide which design in this book you want to tackle. This chapter will help you get started painting it.

1 Transfer the Pattern

Tips for Tracing

- Save time by laying a second thin sheet of tracing paper on top of your tracing paper pattern and using a ballpoint pen to transfer the pattern. This way you'll be able to see which lines you've already traced without marking on your pattern.
- When you've become experienced at painting these designs, you could use just a daisy center to represent a daisy and a circle to represent a rose.
- Do the tracing slightly within the lines and paint over the edge of the tracing, eliminating the need to remove graphite lines from the painting surface.

1 Trace the outline of the area you'll be decorating onto tracing paper by laying a sheet of tracing paper over the surface and etching the outline with a graphite pencil.

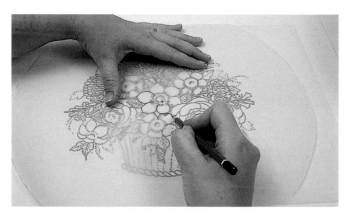

2 Cut this template out and position it over the selected design for perfect placement. Trace the design onto the template with a pencil, making any changes necessary to adapt the design to the shape and size of your surface.

3 Now lay the traced pattern on the piece and secure it with magic tape. Slide a sheet of carbon paper under the tracing paper, shiny side down.

4 Trace the design lightly with a stylus. Lift the edge and check your lines frequently to be sure they're not too dark. Light tracings are easier to remove.

2 Know Your Brushstrokes

Refer to chapter one to learn about round brushes. Practice the strokes described in chapter three on paper.

3 Perfect the Technique

It is important to refer to chapter four often until you become proficient with the multi-loading method.

4 Establish Color Balance

Don't think about color at this stage; instead, concentrate on balance. The best way to explain this concept is to use a triangle and inverted triangle method.

Look at the overall effect of the piece. The colors are balanced and connected by the daisy centers.

This diagram shows how I have balanced the colors—golds, reds and blues—in this project. Refer to the finished project on page 76 for a closer look at the colors.

13 Basic Brushstrokes Overview

B/s 1: Work left to right. Hold the brush at a 45° angle, pressure on the toe, and "pull thread through the needle."

B/s 2: Work right to left. Hold the brush at a 45° angle, pressure on the toe, and "pull thread through the needle."

B/s 3: Hold brush parallel to side of the page, pressure on the toe, lift, quarter-roll and pull action.

B/s 4: Work left to right, lightly pull, stop, pressure and immediately conclude as for b/s 1.

B/s 5: Work right to left, lightly pull, stop, pressure and immediately conclude as for b/s 2.

B/s 6: Start lightly at the left, gradually apply pressure toward the heel, drag to the right and lift.

B/s 7: Start lightly at the right, gradually apply pressure toward the heel, drag to the left and lift.

B/s 8: As for b/s 3, start lightly on the toe, gradually apply pressure to the left, lift, roll and pull.

B/s 9: As for b/s 3, start lightly on the toe, gradually apply pressure to the right, lift, roll and pull.

B/s 10: As for b/s 3, start lightly on the toe, gradually apply pressure to the page, lift, roll and pull.

B/s 11: Start lightly, apply gradual pressure at the waist of the C and gradually lift as you end the stroke.

B/s 12: As for b/s 11, but in the opposite direction.

B/s 13: At 45° angle, apply pressure to the toe, move to the right and repeat with more pressure; keep moving to the right and retain the brush angle at 45°.

Photocopy and laminate this bookmark for quick reference.

5 Color Placement

When choosing colors, mark them on the tracing, keeping in mind that prominent flowers should carry the major color. Choose a complementing color for the chrysanthemums and basket, and be sure to carry this color through in some daisy centers. The third color is often blue, unless the design is being painted on a blue background. Blue seems to enhance and lift the overall appearance of the colors in a piece. Choose color wisely, and adapt it to suit your background. Make the most of your foliage color. I usually continue the background color into the foliage wherever possible, as in project three.

As an example of how to read a design, I've marked the following elements on this pattern:
- Washes are marked in stippled lines.
- Darkest foliage is marked in blue.
- Medium foliage is marked in red.
- Remaining foliage is marked in green (these are usually finishing foliage and for the most part the lightest).

6 Paint the Foliage

- Always start with the elements furthest away and work forward.
- Light and dark backgrounds are treated differently. Follow the instructions carefully.
- All foliage is not seen straight on; sometimes leaves turn or appear at an angle, drop back or lean forward.
- Attempt to keep the characteristics of foliage appropriate—rose leaves for roses and tulip leaves for tulips.
- Study the foliage and establish how the leaves relate to the flowers and their direction. Remember that the pattern is merely a guideline and does not require exact duplication. I am well known for the quote: "The pattern is merely an indication, not a stipulation." When you like your brushstroke, even if it doesn't resemble mine, leave it alone! Remember, I am teaching you to do your *own* painting. I merely set the guidelines.

7 Paint the Flowers

- Start with major flowers—generally these carry the dominant color.
- The secondary flowers carry a complementary color.
- A contrasting color is used for the smallest flowers.
- If additional flowers are used, either repeat a color that needs to be carried, or add a neutral color such as white.

8 Finishing the Work

Consider whether you want to patina your piece. (Instructions are given on page 139.) If you do not patina, remove the tracing lines. If patina treatment is chosen, *do not* erase tracing lines. The patina medium will resist penetrating the area erased, creating an irreversible blotchy background. Patina can be important, particularly when painting traditional designs with bright colors. Your work is now ready to be sealed.

Painting Folk Art Flowers With Enid Hoessinger

Chapter Nine
Color and Abbreviations

For many people it might be daunting having to mix two colors to achieve another—I guess it has to do with that unknown quantity. To make it easier for you, the color reference for each project will indicate the approximate proportions used and the resultant color for both foliage and floral choices. The dots will indicate the proportions of color; for instance, one white dot means to add one part white paint to a mixture. Acrylic bottles make it easy to squeeze out small quantities of paint for mixing.

Color Abbreviations

AG	Antique Green	LB	Lamp Black
AGD	Antique Gold Deep	OB	Oxblood
BG	Blue Green	TB	True Blue
BR	Brilliant Red	TW	Titanium White
BU	Burnt Umber	YL	Yellow Light

Other Abbreviations

B	blue mix	and	colors should be mixed together on the palette
CC	contrast color		
MDC	main daisy color	+	a plus sign means lift or sweep the color, allowing the colors to mix on the brush during the application of strokes
MFC	main foliage color		
MRC	main rose color		
MTC	main tulip color		

White Paint

It's very important to reduce the viscosity of Titanium White by adding 1 teaspoon of distilled water for every 2 oz. bottle. Shake it well.

Palette Tip

For a large project you could have two palettes, one for foliage colors and one for flower colors. This way you can keep the foliage colors laid out until the flowers are completed so you can return to paint veins, leaves overlapping flowers and other finishing touches.

Color
Suggestions

These pages show traditional background colors with samples of foliage and floral colors. A multitude of floral and foliage colors can be achieved using my range of colors. As limiting as that range may seem, all the projects in this book have been created with these colors. I've provided some suggestions of colors. Try these combinations when you have exhausted the color palettes given with each project. Have fun mixing them. All foliage and flower colors shown here will also work well on a black background.

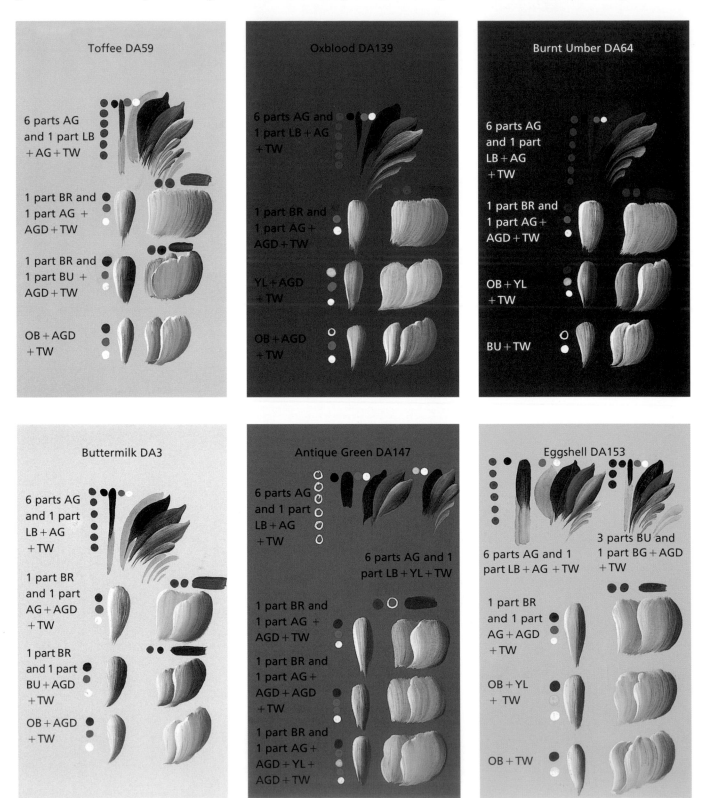

Toffee DA59

6 parts AG and 1 part LB +AG +TW

1 part BR and 1 part AG + AGD +TW

1 part BR and 1 part BU + AGD +TW

OB + AGD +TW

Oxblood DA139

6 parts AG and 1 part LB + AG +TW

1 part BR and 1 part AG + AGD +TW

YL + AGD +TW

OB + AGD +TW

Burnt Umber DA64

6 parts AG and 1 part LB + AG +TW

1 part BR and 1 part AG + AGD +TW

OB + YL +TW

BU +TW

Buttermilk DA3

6 parts AG and 1 part LB + AG +TW

1 part BR and 1 part AG + AGD +TW

1 part BR and 1 part BU + AGD +TW

OB + AGD +TW

Antique Green DA147

6 parts AG and 1 part LB + AG +TW

6 parts AG and 1 part LB + YL +TW

1 part BR and 1 part AG + AGD +TW

1 part BR and 1 part AG + AGD + AGD +TW

1 part BR and 1 part AG + AGD + YL + AGD +TW

Eggshell DA153

6 parts AG and 1 part LB + AG +TW

3 parts BU and 1 part BG + AGD +TW

1 part BR and 1 part AG + AGD +TW

OB + YL + TW

OB + TW

Painting Folk Art Flowers With Enid Hoessinger

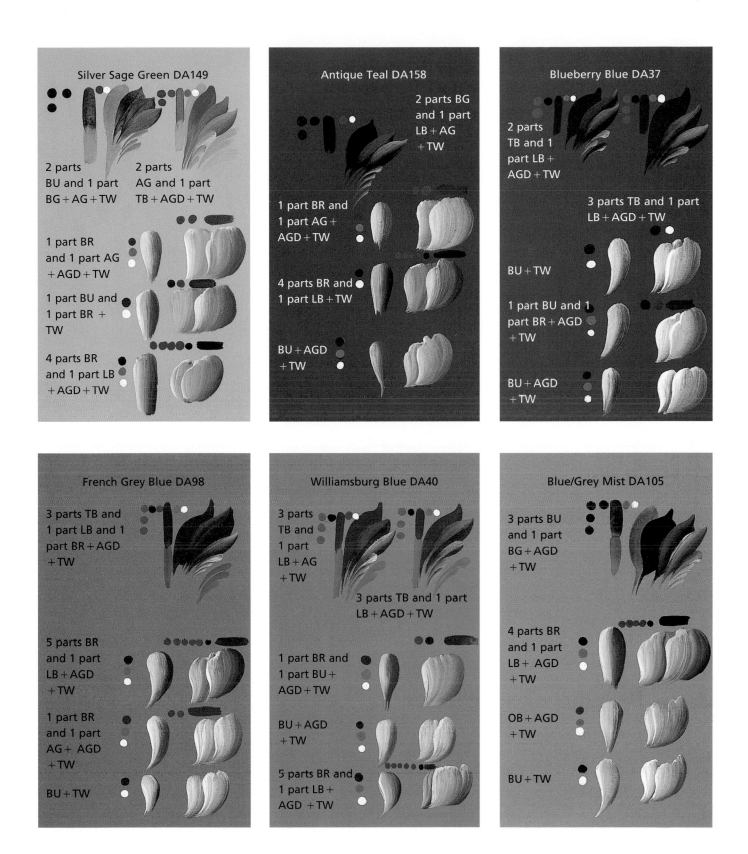

Silver Sage Green DA149

2 parts
BU and 1 part
BG + AG + TW

2 parts
AG and 1 part
TB + AGD + TW

1 part BR
and 1 part AG
+ AGD + TW

1 part BU and
1 part BR +
TW

4 parts BR
and 1 part LB
+ AGD + TW

Antique Teal DA158

2 parts BG
and 1 part
LB + AG
+ TW

1 part BR and
1 part AG +
AGD + TW

4 parts BR and
1 part LB + TW

BU + AGD
+ TW

Blueberry Blue DA37

2 parts
TB and 1
part LB +
AGD + TW

3 parts TB and 1 part
LB + AGD + TW

BU + TW

1 part BU and 1
part BR + AGD
+ TW

BU + AGD
+ TW

French Grey Blue DA98

3 parts TB and
1 part LB and 1
part BR + AGD
+ TW

5 parts BR
and 1 part
LB + AGD
+ TW

1 part BR
and 1 part
AG + AGD
+ TW

BU + TW

Williamsburg Blue DA40

3 parts
TB and
1 part
LB + AG
+ TW

3 parts TB and 1 part
LB + AGD + TW

1 part BR and
1 part BU +
AGD + TW

BU + AGD
+ TW

5 parts BR and
1 part LB +
AGD + TW

Blue/Grey Mist DA105

3 parts BU
and 1 part
BG + AGD
+ TW

4 parts BR
and 1 part
LB + AGD
+ TW

OB + AGD
+ TW

BU + TW

Pink Hatbox

This design, extracted from the gable, or crown, of the schrank shown on page 7, has slight asymmetrical touches. It will happily suit a plate or other round object, or even a square. Prepare and basecoat the project as described on pages 54–55 and transfer the pattern from page 77 as shown on page 56. Paint the basket first, followed by the washes, the darkest foliage, the medium foliage, the flowers, the filler foliage, and the extended washes. Finally, finish the box with sponging. (The sponging technique is demonstrated on page 112.)

Brush-loading Problems

Problem: I have too much AGD in my brush.
Solution: Do not sweep through a puddle of paint; instead, sweep over some pulled-out color.

Problem: My brush is dry.
Solution: You must sweep through enough paint when reloading to sufficiently load the brush—strike a happy medium.

Palette

Background
Mix 1 part Dusty Rose DA25 and 1 part Titanium White

Sponging
French Mocha DA188

Basket and Chrysanthemums
Antique Gold Deep + Burnt Umber + Titanium White (reduced viscosity)

Foliage

Mix 6 parts Antique Green and 1 part Lamp Black = Main Foliage Color (MFC)

MFC + Antique Gold Deep + Titanium White

Roses and Trumpet Flowers
Mix 1 part Brilliant Red and 1 part Burnt Umber (this is the main rose color or MRC) + Antique Green + Titanium White

Large and Small Blue Daisies
Mix 3 parts True Blue and 1 part MRC (this mix is the main daisy color or MDC) and Titanium White + Titanium White

White Daisies
Titanium White + MFC and Lamp Black

THE BASKET

The base is completed in eleven strokes, without basecoating (more strokes are permissible). Read through the steps and practice the necessary strokes on paper. This exercise emphasizes color and stroke control. Gradation of the strokes is crucial. Instructions must be followed to the letter. Follow the steps, working on alternating sides of the basket after the initial stroke.

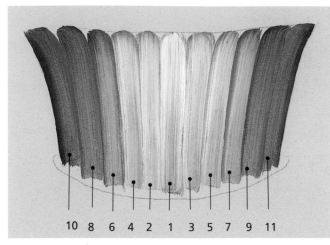

1 Load a no. 5 sable brush in AGD (see sidebar, page 63). *Do not clean the brush between strokes.* Double-load by lifting a good amount of TW away from the puddle. Face the white down to the palette and sweep 12 times through TW in short strokes. (This action will push the paint into the brush, further filling it.) Turn the brush over and sweep the AGD side once firmly in a clean spot on the palette—this a strike-back. Start in the center of the basket, with TW face down. Splay the brush to the required width; move your hand down to paint a brushstroke three, with a slight release of pressure toward the base of the stroke (narrowing it slightly). Use this same stroke for steps 2-11, reloading as directed.

2 Sweep twice through TW on the white side; turn the brush over and sweep once through AGD. Apply with TW face down, left of the first stroke.

3 Repeat step 2 on the right of the first stroke.

4 Sweep once through TW and twice through AGD. Apply.

5 Repeat step 4 for the opposite side.

6 Sweep through AGD four or five times on AGD side. Then, on the same side, sweep several short strokes through a little pulled-out BU. Apply.

7 Repeat step 6 for opposite side, regardless of the amount of BU left on the brush.

8 This time sweep the light side through AGD two or three times and through a little BU on the dark side. Apply.

9 Repeat step 8 for the opposite side.

10 Reload AGD once, sweep through a little more BU (according to required darkness) and apply it in a side-load manner, with dark to the outer side.

11 Repeat step 10 for opposite side. Now you can clean your brush!

12 To smooth out the bottom edge, load a Habico 122AF no. 4 brush in AGD and sweep through BU. Hold AGD face down and pull a medium-pressure stroke into the center from both sides. Allow this to dry.

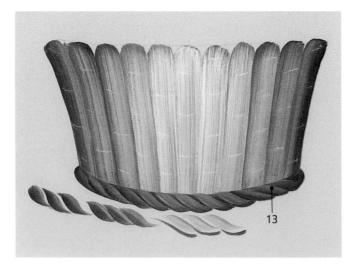

Painting Folk Art Flowers With Enid Hoessinger

13 To paint the twisted weave around the bottom, load the brush in AGD, lift only a little TW, and sweep once on the white side. Sweep back on AGD side before sweeping through a little pulled-out BU. Work from right to left, making an S-stroke with a plump waist. The stroke should be lighter when you reach the center. The tricky part is to get each stroke darker as you move away from the center—this requires a strike-back and, for more intense darkening, a short sweep through a little more BU each time. Add a little highlight where needed and a little dark for shadow. Allow to dry. Use chalk to lightly mark guidelines for the basket weave.

14 For the pattern on the basket, double-load the brush in a little AGD and BU—the brush should barely have paint in it. Flatten the brush to a knife-edge. Paint from the bottom up and toward the center without cleaning the brush; the BU will diminish and the AGD will carry sufficient contrast. Repeat for the opposite side.

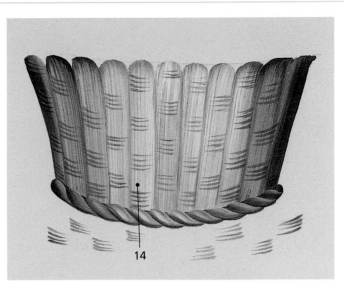

FOLIAGE

Use a no. 3 brush for all foliage work. Refer to chapter four to refresh your knowledge of foliage procedure. To help you out, I have marked the washes on the pattern in stippled lines. Never trace these lines. The strokes to paint rose leaves are demonstrated on pages 30–31. Daisy leaves are demonstrated below.

1 Start with a wash. Note the direction the center foliage faces. Build up dry washes in the middle of the design where the foliage is denser. Blot excess watery paint from the palette and brush.

2 Block out the darkest underlying foliage (marked in blue on the pattern) with the main foliage color. Watch the balance.

3 Medium foliage (marked in red on the pattern) is done with a double load of the main foliage color plus AGD, with the main purpose being to overlap leaves and create movement. Refer to chapter four.

4 With a light background, a triple load is not effective on the outer areas. You will need to embellish the lightest foliage (marked in green on the pattern) toward the center of the design, leaving those leaves that overlap the flowers for later.

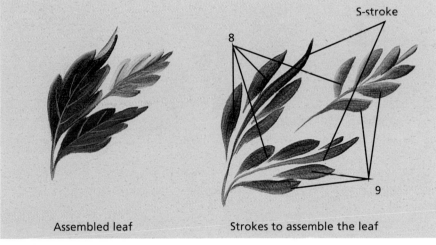

Assembled leaf   Strokes to assemble the leaf

Daisy Leaves
With the main foliage color in the brush, paint an S-stroke in the middle. Add brushstroke eight to the left and brushstroke nine to the right. Keep the light side of a double and triple load to the outside of the leaf. Work from the base to the tip, with good pressure for each stroke as they merge in the center.

DABBLED ROSE CENTER

The following roses will give you an idea of the procedure so you will be able to paint a variety of roses by yourself. In general:

• Start at the beginning of the rose and continue through all the strokes without washing the brush.

• For a deeper tone, sweep through a little dark on the dark side. For a lighter tone, sweep through the TW on the light side.

• The colors will become distorted while painting the center and should remain in the brush. There is no need to reload the brush, other than to lighten or darken a color when instructed.

• Left-handed painters should work in the opposite direction.

• Vary the centers by altering their shape from round to oval. A multitude of roses can be painted by starting in this way.

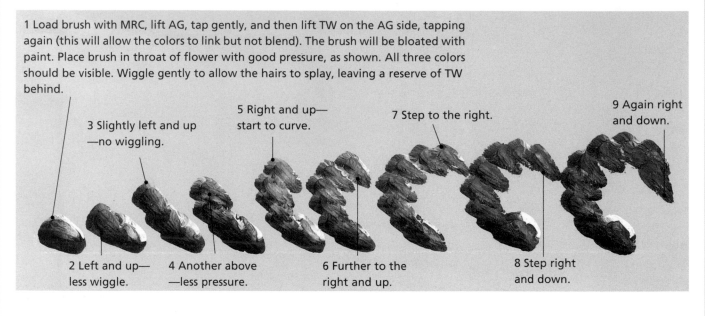

1 Load brush with MRC, lift AG, tap gently, and then lift TW on the AG side, tapping again (this will allow the colors to link but not blend). The brush will be bloated with paint. Place brush in throat of flower with good pressure, as shown. All three colors should be visible. Wiggle gently to allow the hairs to splay, leaving a reserve of TW behind.

3 Slightly left and up —no wiggling.

5 Right and up— start to curve.

7 Step to the right.

9 Again right and down.

2 Left and up— less wiggle.

4 Another above —less pressure.

6 Further to the right and up.

8 Step right and down.

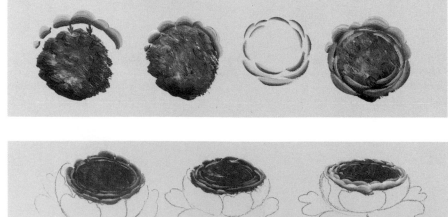

10 Continue to move down and to the left, closing the circle in a spiraled manner by tapping into the TW left behind (which will feed the brush) so the final stipple in the middle is the same, but smaller. The colors should distort to create a mottled glow in the center.

11 The brush may now be dry and scruffy looking. Reload by sweeping the dark side in a little dark paint and lifting a small amount of secondhand white. Paint a series of brushstroke thirteens, attached to the top of the center, with the TW facing away. Re-tip a little TW and face it toward the center to paint small brushstrokes one and two. Note the comma strokes in the front, lying on the dark patch of the center—try to paint some of these to create depth.

These are examples of oval centers, used mainly for roses at different angles.

Painting Folk Art Flowers With Enid Hoessinger

HORIZONTAL-STROKE ROSE ONE

This rose begins with the dabbled rose center shown at left. Do not clean the brush after completing the center.

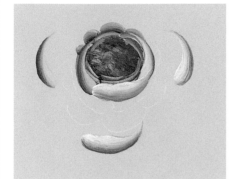 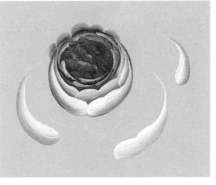 

1 Paint the center. Now turn the work upside down and, with a little increased secondhand TW, paint a brushstroke one and two on either side, as illustrated. Turn the rose to the left and follow up with a double brushstroke two (pressure-lift, pressure-lift).

2 Increase the white for each stroke, still upside down. Add brushstrokes one and two, this time shifting the strokes a little to create alternating petals.

3 Darken the brush by sweeping once over AG on the dark side, and then sweep through MRC on the same side. Block in outer petals using brushstroke thirteen (see variation below.)

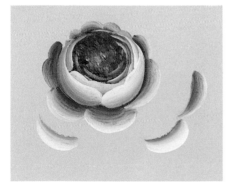 

5 The finished horizontal-stroke rose one. Clean the brush and start again for the next rose center.

4 Increase TW. Add a brushstroke thirteen on top of the three front petals painted in step 3.

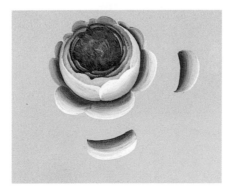

Variation on Step 3
Complete step 2, darken the brush by sweeping once over AG on the dark side, and then sweep through the MRC. Paint the distant side petals using brushstroke thirteen. Increase TW only, turn the rose upside-down, hold the dark against the rose and push firmly toward the white for front petals.

HORIZONTAL-STROKE ROSE TWO

This rose is painted in the same way as the first horizontal-stroke rose, beginning with a dabbled rose center. To create a slightly larger rose, brush-stroke two in the front was enlarged by repeating the push-and-lift action three times. This creates more space between side petals, which also gives the rose a different look. Slowly increase the white to create gradually lighter petals.

1 Turn the work to the left for brushstroke one, immediately followed by a triple brushstroke one. On the opposite side, paint a double brushstroke two.

2 Increase white slowly for each stroke. Turn the work to the side for the center stroke and upside down for the side strokes.

3 Sweep back through a little AG, and then MRC. Paint an outer petal on either side and increase the white for the front petals.

4 Sweep several times through TW—only then paint the upper section of the final front petal. Immediately paint the lower section, slightly overlapping.

5 The horizontal-stroke rose two assembled. Clean the brush to start the next rose.

Painting Folk Art Flowers With Enid Hoessinger

C-STROKE ROSE

Start with the dabbled rose center, but leave off the final comma strokes.

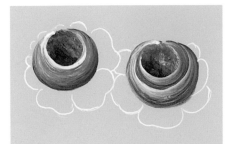

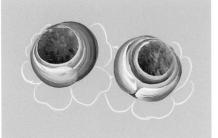

1 Start with the dabbled rose center. Load clean TW, face it to the center of the mouth, turn the work sideways and, while holding the brush perpendicular, paint a tight C-stroke. To paint a larger flower, as shown on the right, add a second C-stroke.

2 Increase TW, turn the work upside down and paint a single brushstroke one—add brushstroke two if necessary.

3 Paint small brushstroke one—and two, if necessary—in the center.

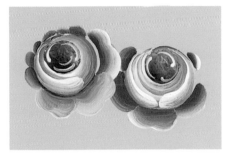

4 Darken the brush and paint the outer petals (brushstroke thirteen) toward the back of the rose and the underlying petals. Increase TW for lighter petals.

5 Add two thin petals (like brushstrokes eleven and twelve with pressure toward the inner side) between the bowl and the outer skirt. Add turn-backs.

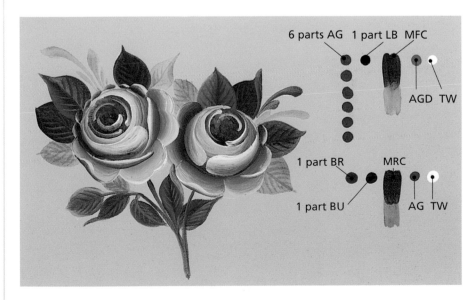

6 parts AG   1 part LB   MFC

AGD   TW

1 part BR   MRC

1 part BU   AG   TW

6 C-stroke rose assembled, with accompanying foliage.

CHRYSANTHEMUMS

The entire flower is painted with
brushstrokes one, two and three.

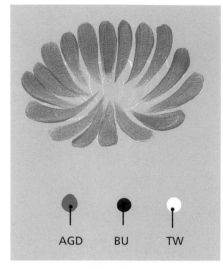

1 With a single load of AGD, block out
the outer row of petals.

2 Replace AGD, sweep through a little
BU and paint another stroke, slightly
smaller, with the AGD face down inside
each stroke. Sweep through small amounts
of BU as often as needed.

3 Add half a row of smaller AGD strokes,
alternating inside.

4 Repeat step 2 and then clean the brush.

5 Double-load with AGD and TW. Strike back before each
stroke. Holding white down, paint brushstroke three in the center, brushstroke one to the right and brushstroke two to the left.
Repeat brushstroke one and two on either side again, sweeping back
through AGD.

Painting Folk Art Flowers With Enid Hoessinger

6 Repeat step 5 with increased TW, taking it a little further around.

7 For the second layer of outer petals, turn the work upside down, replace TW, hold it to the ceiling and paint brushstroke three. Alternate to paint brushstrokes one and two. TW will automatically fall into place.

8 Cap the petals (as for turn-backs) with a triple load.

9 Increase TW and hold it facing the ceiling for the final five petals.

WHITE DAISIES

The petals are painted with brush-strokes one, two and three.

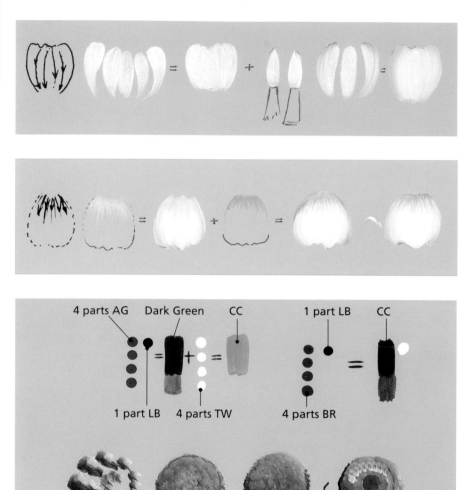

4 parts AG   Dark Green   CC   1 part LB   CC

1 part LB   4 parts TW   4 parts BR

1 Block each petal out in TW. Let it dry. With TW in the brush, sweep only the tip through a little lightened foliage color, and then splay the brush with the dark color to the outside of each petal.

2 Complete all petals, and then darken slightly and pull short knife-edge strokes away from the center to add depth. Increase dark and pull shorter knife-edge strokes over the top for extra depth.

3 Centers are done with a double load of MRC and white, in a similar but more compact motion than dabbled rose centers. Finally, tap a little extra dark in the center, underlining it with MRC.

Here's what the petals should look like prior to adding the center. Add a few turn-backs where desired.

4 The finished white daisy.

BLUE DAISIES

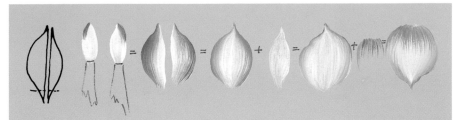

1 Start with the lightest petals. Load with TW, sweep a little blue on one side and paint brushstrokes eight and nine (for narrow petals) with the blue to the outside. For wider petals, paint brushstrokes eight and nine with a gap in the middle and fill it in with brushstroke ten, white face down. Replace TW for each petal and lift small amounts of blue. The brush will darken quickly if care is not taken. Work toward the darker side.

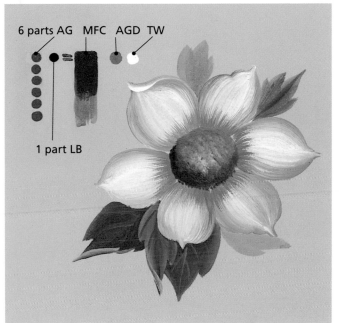

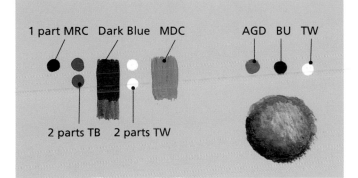

2 Centers are filled with gold and then a side load of BU. Tap around the base for depth. Clean the brush, double-load in gold and white, and tap across the upper side for highlights.

3 Here is the completed blue daisy.

To paint petals falling down at the back of the daisy, sweep the brush firmly through blue (strike-back). Apply first half of brush stroke eleven or twelve, holding white under. This technique may require practice.

SMALL BLUE DAISIES

These daisies are painted in the same manner as project three, with narrower petals.

1 Use an old brush with a blunt tip. Double-load the brush with blue plus TW and sweep back for underlying petals, with white face down.

2 Reload TW, hold white facing the ceiling for all overlapping and lightest petals.

3 Strike back for balance of petals, increasing blue when necessary.

PINK TRUMPET FLOWERS

These trumpet flowers are painted in
the same manner as project three,
with slightly larger petals.

1 With an old brush, double-load with MRC plus TW; sweep
back on MRC for each trumpet using brushstroke three.

2 Continue to sweep back for the dark petals.

3 Lift and tap TW. Hold white facing the ceiling for all lightest
petals.

You may now return to your good brush to add leaves in triple loading, overlap leaves onto flowers, join stems not connected and add small leaves. Finally add washes, tendrils and finishing touches where needed to the outer edge of the design.

Sponging can be done before or after the design is completed.

Painting Folk Art Flowers With Enid Hoessinger

Enlarge pattern to 125% for actual size.

Heirloom Box With Festoons

*T*his design is again extracted from one of the festoons on the gable, or crown, of the schrank on page 7. Prepare and base-coat the project as described on pages 54–55, and transfer the pattern from page 83 as shown on page 56. Paint the foliage first, using a no. 3 brush and the suggested colors; refer to chapter four for foliage procedure. Next paint the unfolding rose, and then refer to project one to paint the chrysanthemums, white daisies, large blue daisies, small blue daisies and trumpet flowers.

Palette

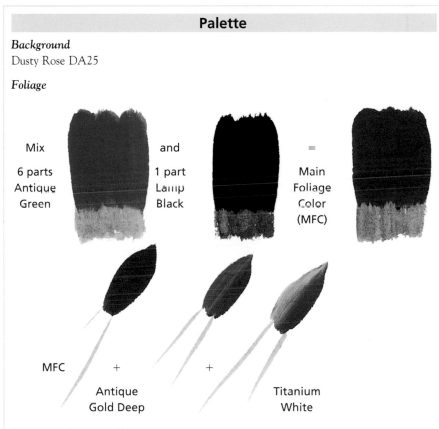

Background
Dusty Rose DA25

Foliage

Mix 6 parts Antique Green and 1 part Lamp Black = Main Foliage Color (MFC)

MFC + Antique Gold Deep + Titanium White

Roses and Trumpet Flowers
4 parts Brilliant Red and 1 part Lamp Black (MRC) + Antique Gold + Titanium White

Chrysanthemums
Antique Gold Deep + Burnt Umber + Titanium White

Large and Small Blue Daisies
3 parts True Blue and 1 part MRC (this mix becomes the MDC) and Titanium White + Titanium White

White Daisies
TW + 4 parts Antique Green and 1 part Lamp Black and 4 parts Titanium White (CC)

Gold Medallions
Antique Gold Deep base
Burnt Umber for contrast
Titanium White highlights

UNFOLDING ROSE

Refer to project one (page 66) to paint the dabbled rose center. Don't wash the brush—it will be scruffy when you are finished with the center, so reload it by sweeping once through a little AG, and then through MRC. Tip the brush with white, tap it gently and continue with the steps below. Turn the rose upside down for brushstrokes one and two.

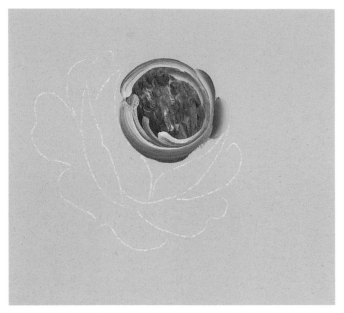

1 Paint the dabbled rose center. Reload the brush as instructed above, and then paint a series of brushstrokes one and two around the entire center.

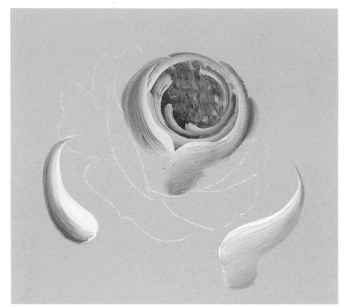

2 Reload the white only and paint brushstrokes one and two. The latter is extended by walking the brush down toward the dark in short strokes like brushstroke three, filling the gap.

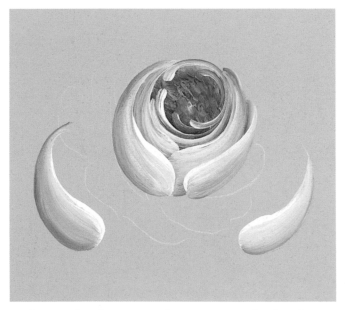

3 Increase the white again and repeat two more brushstrokes one and two.

4 Reload and darken by sweeping once through AG and then firmly through MRC. Paint brushstroke one on the right and brushstroke two twice (overlapping) on the left, followed up by a brushstroke one just below. Increase TW only and paint a plump S-stroke, and then walk the brush back with pressure to merge with brushstroke one.

5 Sweep several times through TW to lighten the brush. Turn the work for brushstroke thirteen. Follow up with another stroke to merge with the first.

6 Reload the white for the final outer petal painted in a double brushstroke—pressure-lift, pressure-lift. Add a turn-back, if justified.

7 For the in-between petal, strike back on the palette and reload TW. Paint brushstroke eleven combined with brushstroke nine in pressure-lift, pressure-lift manner. It's easier than it sounds!

8 Assembled unfolding rose with supporting foliage.

GOLD MEDALLIONS

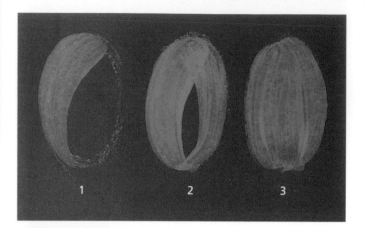

1 Block in medallion with a 1-2-3 brush-stroke in AGD only.

2 To create the highlight, double-load the AGD brush with white. Hold the brush with white facing down to paint brushstroke one on the light side. Clean the brush.

3 To shade the dark side, double-load a brush with AGD + BU. Paint a stroke like a brushstroke two on the side opposite the highlight.

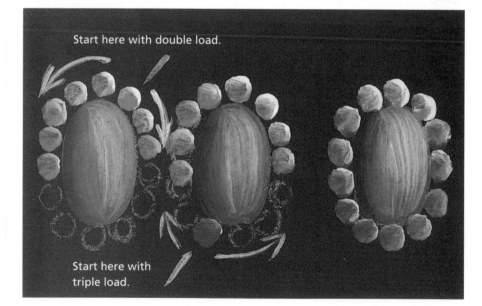

Start here with double load.

Start here with triple load.

4 To paint the dots, double-load the brush with AG + TW. Direct the white toward one o'clock. Start the dots where indicated, and work in the direction of the arrows. Triple-load the same brush by adding a little more AGD, and then BU, to the gold side of the brush. Start the shadowed dots where indicated, and work in the direction of the arrows.

Painting Folk Art Flowers With Enid Hoessinger

Enlarge pattern to 126% for actual size.

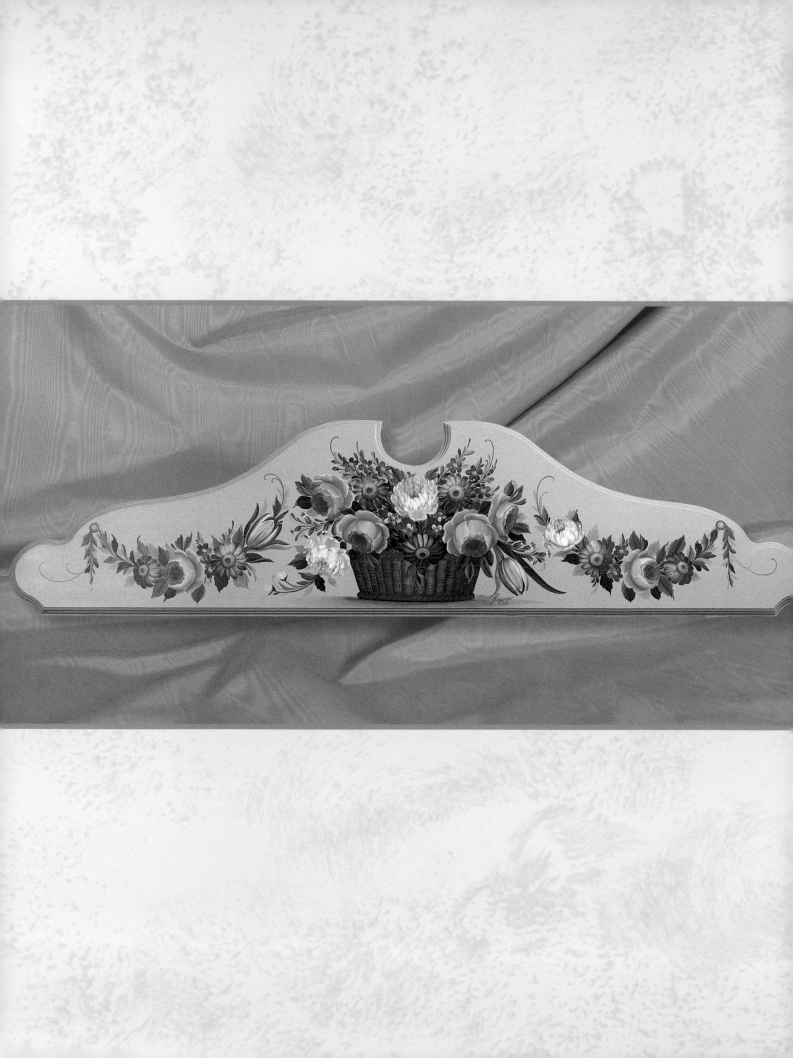

24 Carat Gold Roses on a Door Crown

These roses appear on the gable of the schrank on page 7. Note the asymmetrical treatment of the door crown, and how the placement of white flowers and tulips creates an overall sense of balance. The festoons on either side could be used separately, but the remaining design would need to be revised for balance. The blue-green foliage mix complements the Silver Sage Green background. The gold rose color carries the basket color and continues in the daisy centers for color balance. Pink daisies complement the gold, and the tulips are a combination of the two colors. The design is played down with white peonies, and lifted by a flurry of blue filler flowers.

Prepare and basecoat the project as described on pages 54–55, and transfer the patterns from pages 96 and 97 as shown on page 56. Reverse the pattern on page 97 for the right side. Refer to project one to paint the basket, but use less white to create a darker basket. Paint the foliage next, using either a no. 3 or a no. 4 brush—refer to chapter four for foliage procedure. Do *not* wash the brush for the duration of the foliage painting.

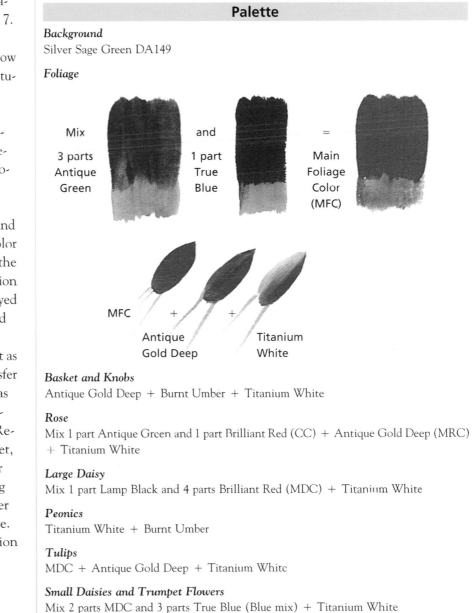

Palette

Background
Silver Sage Green DA149

Foliage

Mix 3 parts Antique Green and 1 part True Blue = Main Foliage Color (MFC)

MFC + Antique Gold Deep + Titanium White

Basket and Knobs
Antique Gold Deep + Burnt Umber + Titanium White

Rose
Mix 1 part Antique Green and 1 part Brilliant Red (CC) + Antique Gold Deep (MRC) + Titanium White

Large Daisy
Mix 1 part Lamp Black and 4 parts Brilliant Red (MDC) + Titanium White

Peonies
Titanium White + Burnt Umber

Tulips
MDC + Antique Gold Deep + Titanium White

Small Daisies and Trumpet Flowers
Mix 2 parts MDC and 3 parts True Blue (Blue mix) + Titanium White

Daisy Centers
Antique Gold Deep + Burnt Umber + Titanium White

24 CARAT
GOLD ROSES

Most people like roses, so I have illustrated many varieties for you to multiply. Use a no. 4 brush.

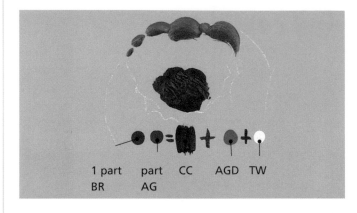

1 part	part	CC	AGD	TW
BR	AG			

1 Start the mouth of the rose by mixing a small amount of CC. Roll the excess off and dabble a reserve of color for the throat. Immediately double-load with AGD and push an irregular brushstroke thirteen in a curve at the top.

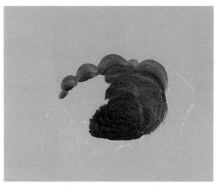

2 Walk brushstroke thirteens down toward the reserve of wet color.

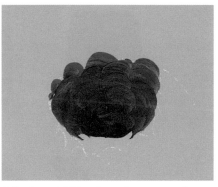

3 Replace AGD only and repeat on the opposite side.

4 Flatten the brush on the dark side and tip a little AGD on the gold side for the small commas in the mouth. Lift a little TW, tap it gently, and paint several brushstrokes one and two in the front. Paint the rose bowl using white sparingly.

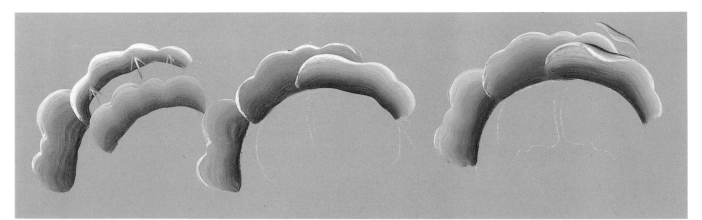

5 Reload the brush with AGD and a good amount of TW, and then sweep the dark side of the brush first through AGD and then through CC (multi-load). Direct the white outward, using three to four brushstroke thirteens. Follow up with maximum pressure to splay the brush outward; keep the same action, but against the rose. Repeat this for all petals. The distant side petals can be painted afterward, using brushstrokes one and two, by sweeping the brush through the CC only—this should yield dark petals.

Painting Folk Art Flowers With Enid Hoessinger

For the second rose, use the same procedures as before, but paint brushstroke thirteen with less curve.

Assembled 24 carat gold roses with supporting foliage.

PINK DAISIES

This strong color lifts the entire design with a pleasing contrast. Brushstroke threes without tails are used—sometimes with a slight curve—except for the turning daisy, where brushstrokes one and two are needed. Use a no. 3 brush.

1 Mix MDC—which at first will appear too dark—and roll the excess off, and then wipe the brush on a paper towel to eliminate most of the color. Sweep through TW three or four times and strike back on the palette. Hold white facing down and paint the first three petals like brushstroke three (start anywhere). Strike back for each stroke, alternating sides. For increased dark, sweep back through MDC, progressively increasing MDC for the darkest petals. Clean the brush.

2 For the center, load AGD and sweep softly through BU. Start at the base and spiral until complete. Add buds.

3 Intensify the shadow with BU and deepen the hollow. Clean the brush and double-load AGD + TW. With white facing down, tap a crescent to highlight the center. Add the calyx with a small brushstroke three.

Painting Folk Art Flowers With Enid Hoessinger

PEONIES

These are like chrysanthemums, but brushstrokes one and two call for a little more curve, especially in the front. Add small strokes to cap. Use a no. 4 brush.

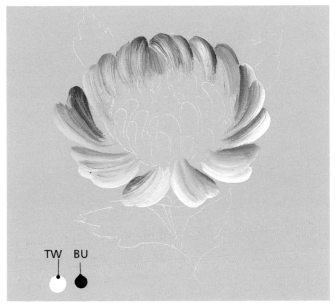

TW   BU

1 Load TW and sweep through BU. Start at the back with brushstroke three in the center, TW down. Replace color as needed and gradually turn the brush to a side load—white to front.

2 Repeat step 1 a little darker. Clean the brush.

3 Load BU. Dabble a little in the center. Add a "smile." Double-load with a little TW held facing the ceiling for inner strokes.

4 Cap the strokes by flattening the dark side and tipping with TW. Hold to the inside of each stroke (like brushstrokes one and two) as per the illustration.

5 Reload as for step 1; strike back for each petal.

6 Increase TW only. With TW facing the surface, turn the brush gradually to the right for each brushstroke one. Reload TW and turn gradually to the left for each brushstroke two. Follow up with smaller strokes between the bowl and outer petals.

Here the front petals are shortened, creating the illusion of looking into the flower.

More petals are added for a fuller flower.

TULIP ONE

A lot of paint is needed in the brush for tulips. For the lighter tulip, brush-strokes eight and nine were used for the center petal. Use a no. 4 brush.

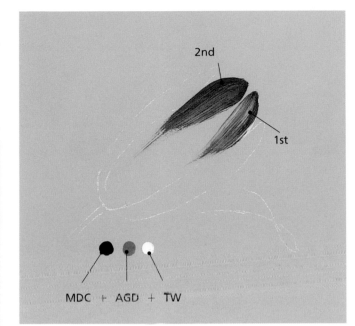

1 Load MDC. Sweep AGD once, TW once, and then turn the brush over and sweep back through MDC. Paint one back petal like brushstrokes one and two, white side down; sweep back and paint second back petal.

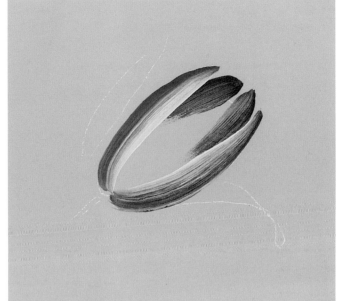

2 Reload, sweeping twice into AGD, twice through TW and sweep back on MDC. Apply a side load to the left; reload and apply to the right.

3 Sweep AGD once and TW four times. Paint brushstroke nine, white to the center.

4 Turn the brush over for brushstroke eight.

TULIP TWO

1 Follow the same approach as before—paint one large stroke for the back petal.

2 Reload, sweeping twice into AGD, twice through TW and sweep back on MDC. Apply a side load to the left; reload and apply to the right.

3 For the center petal, replace AG and sweep into TW four or five times. Sweep back, and then apply brushstroke ten in the middle.

4 Turn the brush fractionally down to the right for brushstroke nine and the opposite direction for brushstroke eight.

5 A little dark color may be added for extra effect, and two small brushstrokes one and two for turn-backs.

Assembled tulip with foliage.

Painting Folk Art Flowers With Enid Hoessinger

SMALL DAISIES

This design can afford a strong blue color, as blue complements the yellow roses very well. Use an old brush with the point worn off.

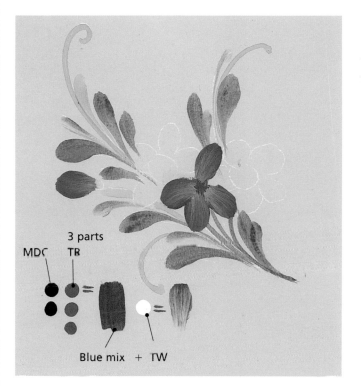

1 Double-load the brush in Blue mix + TW, strike back for each petal and keep white facing down. Paint underlying daisies first using the start of brushstroke three.

2 Double-load TW, this time keeping it facing the ceiling for the overlapping petals. Turn white down for balance of petals. Increase and decrease white for variation.

3 Triple-load the brush in AGD + BU + TW; paint a push-dot (as if to start brushstroke thirteen) in the center.

TRUMPET
FLOWERS
Paint all the petals with an old brush.

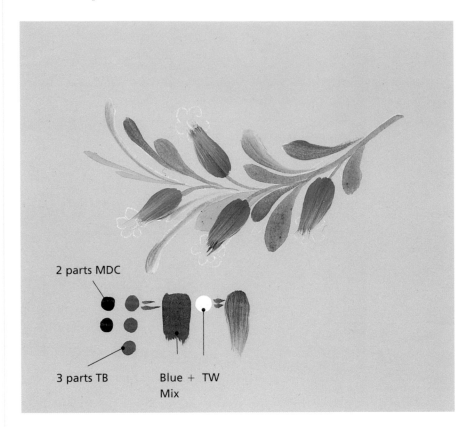

2 parts MDC

3 parts TB

Blue + TW Mix

1 Double-load the brush in Blue mix + TW; sweep back. Hold white down for each brushstroke three and repeat the sweep before each trumpet.

2 Roll off the excess, tip with white and tap brush several times to allow the colors to merge. Paint front petals (as if to start a small brushstroke three) with white facing the ceiling; hold the white down for balance of petals.

3 Paint a plain blue dot in the center.

Painting Folk Art Flowers With Enid Hoessinger

Close-ups of the flowers.

24 Carat Gold Roses on a Door Crown

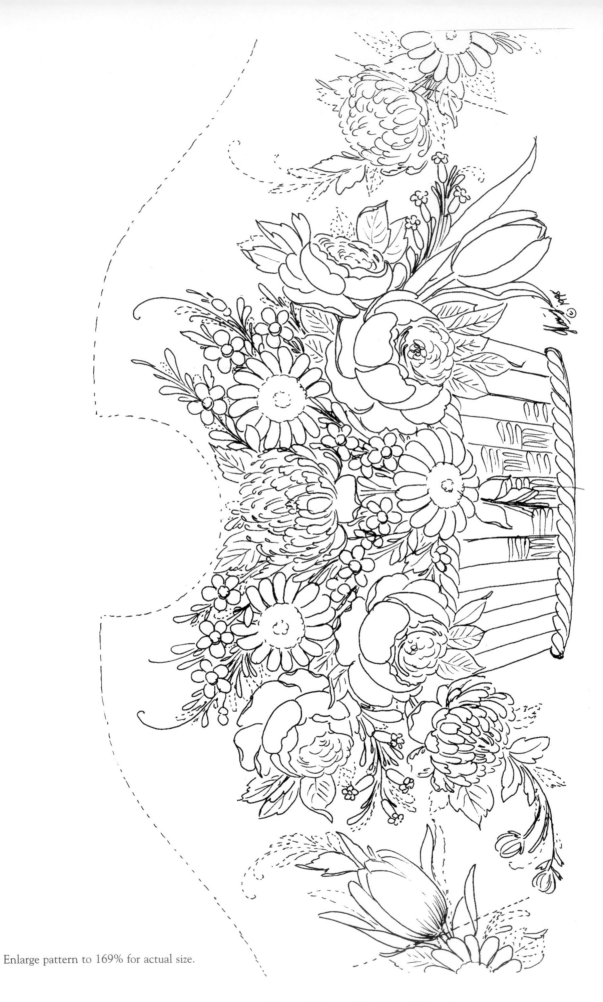

Enlarge pattern to 169% for actual size.

Reverse and repeat
on the opposite side.

Enlarge pattern to 169% for actual size.

Roses Galore on a Door Crown

*I*n this project, again extracted from the gable of the schrank on page 7, I used a large variety of roses to show how such a busy design can be subdued by limiting the colors. The dark background helps to make this possible. The roses and tulips pick up from the background color; even the white anemones continue to reflect the tone. The basket is dark and does not impose on the design, other than picking up the gold within the small roses and flower centers. The blue is kept dark, with only highlights connecting the lighter blue daisies. Prepare and basecoat the project as described on pages 54–55, and transfer the pattern from pages 108 and 109 as shown on page 56. Paint the basket as instructed in project one, using less white to achieve a darker result. Next paint the foliage, and then the large, medium and mini-roses, the large blue daisies and the white anemones. The tulips are painted next; refer to project three. Minor variations can be applied; however, keep them quiet, because this design does not need fancy details. Finish the design with blue star daisies.

Palette

Background
Antique Maroon DA160

Foliage

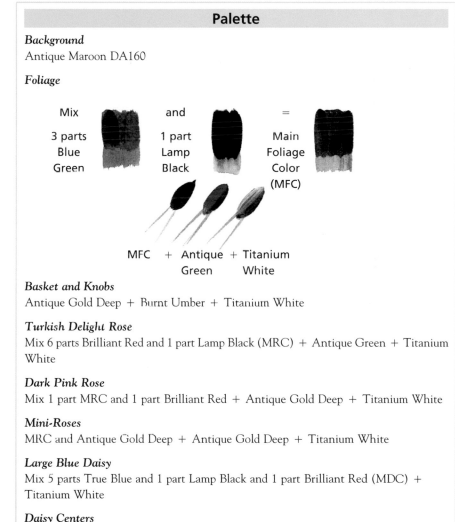

Mix 3 parts Blue Green and 1 part Lamp Black = Main Foliage Color (MFC)

MFC + Antique Green + Titanium White

Basket and Knobs
Antique Gold Deep + Burnt Umber + Titanium White

Turkish Delight Rose
Mix 6 parts Brilliant Red and 1 part Lamp Black (MRC) + Antique Green + Titanium White

Dark Pink Rose
Mix 1 part MRC and 1 part Brilliant Red + Antique Gold Deep + Titanium White

Mini-Roses
MRC and Antique Gold Deep + Antique Gold Deep + Titanium White

Large Blue Daisy
Mix 5 parts True Blue and 1 part Lamp Black and 1 part Brilliant Red (MDC) + Titanium White

Daisy Centers
Antique Gold Deep + Burnt Umber + Titanium White

Anemones
Titanium White + Burnt Umber

Tulips
Mix 1 part MRC and 1 part Brilliant Red (MFC) + Antique Gold Deep + Titanium White

Blue Star Daisies
Mix 1 part MDC and 1 part Titanium White (Blue mix) + Titanium White

FOLIAGE

Paint only the underlying foliage in MFC. Double-load in AG for subtle lightening. For triple-loading, use very little TW to indicate a few leaves catching the light. After the flowers are painted in, the smallest leaves and those overlapping onto flowers should be painted with a *little* more TW. This color mix can turn blue very quickly: Remember to replace the AG before lifting TW. Refer to chapter four for foliage procedure.

Painting Folk Art Flowers With Enid Hoessinger

TURKISH DELIGHT PINK ROSES

Use a no. 3 brush. Paint the larger, light pink, advanced-level roses like the 24 carat gold roses on pages 86 and 87. The only difference is these roses have convex outer skirt petals, which are painted like the anemones on pages 105–106. The colors of these roses require a little more control; they should not lighten up too soon. Start the mouth with MRC and AGD only. The AGD will work itself into the brush. Slowly increase the TW for the first layers of petals by sweeping only the tip of the brush through AGD, and then through a little TW, and then perform a strike-back. Continue to lighten the brush slowly with more TW, creating the Turkish Delight pink. For the skirt, sweep back through AGD before the MRC to darken for the side petals further back, increasing white toward the front.

SMALLER DARK PINK ROSES

Paint the dark pink roses in a similar manner. Keep the mouths small and the outer petals concave.

MINI-ROSES

There are numerous combinations to choose from when painting these mini-roses. Here I've created fifteen different roses just by altering the inside strokes and outer petals—try some variations of your own.

1 Block out entire bowl.

2 Darken center with a little MRC.

3 Build strokes up around the mouth and add different outer petals.

4 Add different inside strokes for variety.

1 Block out entire bowl.

2 Darken center with a little MRC.

3 Build strokes up around the mouth and add different outer petals.

4 Add different inside strokes for variety.

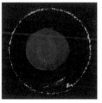 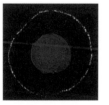   

1 Block out entire bowl.

2 Darken center with a little MRC.

3 Build strokes up around the mouth and add different outer petals.

4 Add different inside strokes for variety.

    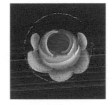

1 Block out entire bowl.

2 Darken center with BU.

3 Build strokes up around the mouth.

4 Add brushstrokes eleven, twelve, one or two.

5 Add different outer petals.

6 Add different inside strokes for variety.

 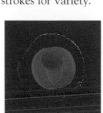 

1 Block out entire bowl.

2 Darken center with BU.

3 Build strokes up around the mouth.

4 Add brushstrokes eleven, twelve, one or two.

5 Add different outer petals.

6 Add different inside strokes for variety.

1 Block out entire bowl.

2 Darken center with BU.

3 Build strokes up around the mouth.

4 Add brushstrokes eleven, twelve, one or two.

5 Add different outer petals.

6 Add different inside strokes for variety.

LARGE BLUE DAISIES

These are painted with brushstrokes one, two and three in any order.

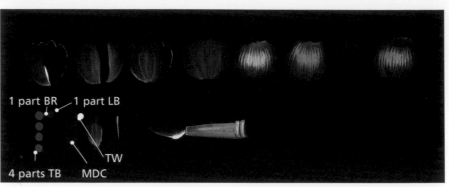

1 Load the brush in MDC, and then lift a dot of white at the heel of the brush. Sweep back in MDC and apply each stroke (brushstrokes one, two and three) with pressure.

2 Reload in the same manner for each stroke until a petal is done. Repeat the procedure for all petals. Do not wash the brush between petals.

3 When all these flowers are done, load with white and paint feathery strokes—allow to dry.

4 Clean the brush and wash over the white with watery blue paint.

5 Reload in MDC and pull short knife-edge brushstrokes from the center.

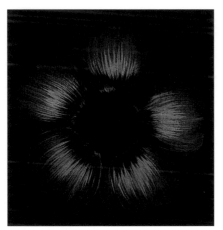

Observe depth and highlight.

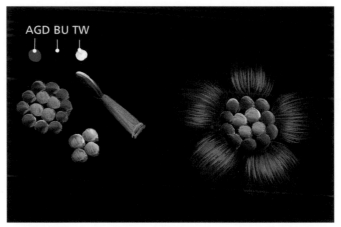

6 Centers are painted with a triple load of AGD + BU + TW. Hold the brush at a 45° angle with all colors visible. Start at the base of each dot, push against the white and then lift sharply. Older brushes without a point are best for these strokes.

BLUE STAR DAISIES

Use brushstroke ten for this daisy, keeping it nice and delicate.

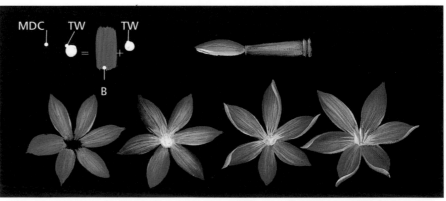

1 Double-load the brush in the Blue mix + TW. Sweep back through the Blue mix for each petal.

2 With small knife-edge brushstrokes, turn some petals.

3 The center is a dot of white—pull knife-edge strokes from the center outward and add brushstrokes one, two and three for the stamen.

Painting Folk Art Flowers With Enid Hoessinger

WHITE ANEMONES

First, notice the difference between the concave and convex petals. These are typical for roses and peonies. Concave petals are dark in the center and light toward the outside; convex petals are light in the center and darker toward the outside.

Concave Petals

 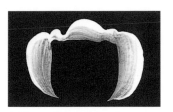  

1 Paint irregular brushstroke thirteens across the top, ending with brushstroke one, light to the outside.

2 Turn white over and paint brushstroke two on the opposite side.

3 Hold dark down and paint brushstroke three in center, walking it out.

4 Repeat on the opposite side.

Convex Petals

1 Paint irregular brushstroke thirteens across the top.

2 Hold the white down and paint brushstroke three in the center, walking it out toward either side, using brushstroke one toward the right, rolling it slightly toward the right for shading.

3 Reload the white if necessary and repeat brushstroke two on the left, again rolling the brush slightly to the left for a darker effect.

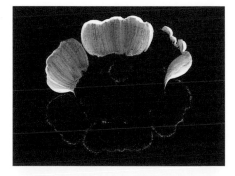

1 Paint the back petal concave.

3 Paint a convex petal in the front. Darken the brush, turn the light side to face the ceiling and add the first row of inner petals with tailless brushstroke tens, turning slightly to show a little light toward the front of each stroke.

2 The side petals gradate from dark at the back to light in the front.

4 Darken the brush and repeat the previous step a little lower.

5 Repeat the previous step a little lower. Cap all petals with knife-edge brushstrokes one, two and three.

6 Lighten the brush by sweeping several times through white. Paint a row of petals from the center to the back on each side, turning the brush to darken the outside of each petal.

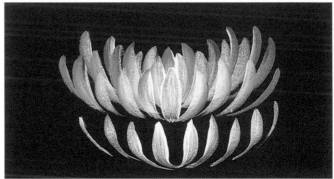

Separated strokes indicate alternating petals in layers.

7 Repeat two more layers in the same way, increasing the white only until completed.

Assembled anemone with supporting foliage.

Roses Galore on a Door Crown 107

Enlarge pattern to 169% for actual size.

Painting Folk Art Flowers With Enid Hoessinger

Enlarge pattern to 169% for actual size.

Roses Galore on a Door Crown

Versatile Storage Box

*T*his practical box can be used in the dining room for napkins, coasters or candles, in the bathroom to store special soap, or in the bedroom for numerous purposes. The design, taken from the side of the schrank on page 7, lends itself to modern decor and is easy to paint.

Prepare and basecoat the project as described on pages 54–55, and transfer the pattern from pages 116 and 117 as shown on page 56. Use the color of your choice for sponging to personalize the box. Foliage is simply painted in one color, slightly thinned. Select the darkest leaves and paint all of them. Make a wash with the paint in the brush to paint the remaining leaves. The chrysanthemums are painted with brushstrokes one, two and three, with brushstroke thirteen skirts. The mini-roses are a series of small C-strokes. The small tulips are painted with brushstrokes eight, nine and ten. The flower in the center is a simple combination of brushstrokes eight, nine and ten, painted in gold, highlighted with a touch of TW and shaded with BU. Add contrast in the center using knife-edge strokes. The scrolls on the side of the box are done in the same manner, keeping the light color to the upper side.

Palette

Background
Buttermilk DA3

Sponging
Violet Haze DA197 (or color of your choice)

Scrolls
Antique Gold Deep + Burnt Umber + Titanium White

Foliage

Mix 2 parts Antique Green   and   1 part True Blue   =   Main Foliage Color (MFC)

MFC   Lighter wash of MFC   Lightest wash of MFC

Flowers
Antique Gold Deep + Burnt Umber + Titanium White

SPONGING

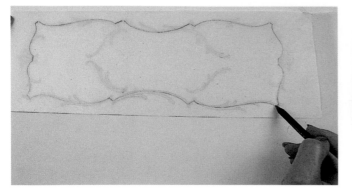

1 Prepare the entire piece, inside and out, with Buttermilk. Transfer the design onto the box. Cut Friskit Film (a light, self-adhesive plastic) to the size of the box lid. Lay the film on the tracing (but do not adhere) and trace a single line along the middle of the scrolls.

2 Cut along this line with a craft knife.

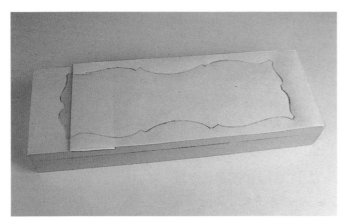

3 Pull the top edge of the Friskit Film backing away from the film and fold it under. Position the edge of the film over the scroll on the box, and then pull the backing off from underneath—this will accurately fit it in place.

4 Wet the sponge, squeeze all the water out and then squeeze it again between paper towels. Thin your favorite paint color in a saucer with a little water. Work a little paint into a coarse part of the sponge. Rapidly sponge evenly on the top and sides of the lid.

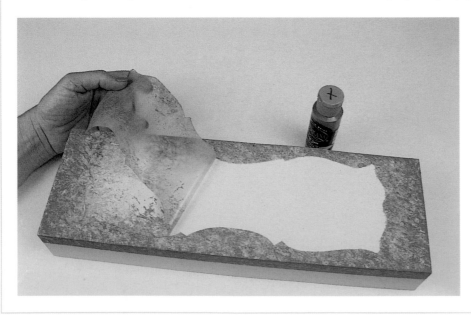

5 Carefully remove the template.

SCROLLS

1 Block the scrolls out in AGD only, painting single strokes by holding the brush almost perpendicular, especially in the curves. Use even, light pressure for the entire stroke. Do not start with pressure.

2 Double-load with AGD and BU. Direct BU to the front of the box for all scrolls (gold side of the brush to gold side of the scroll). Clean the brush. Note the light source coming from one direction.

SCROLLS *(continued)*

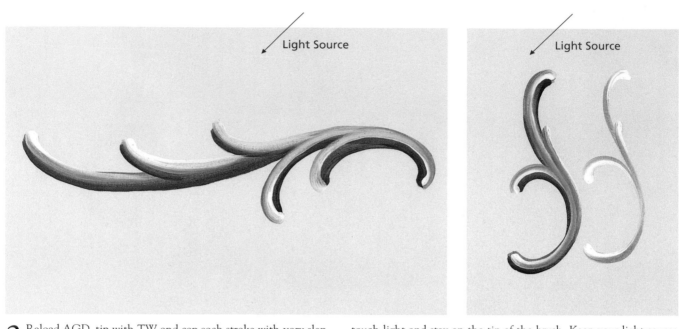

Light Source

Light Source

3 Reload AGD, tip with TW and cap each stroke with very slender strokes, holding the TW toward the inside of the curve of every stroke while painting either brushstroke one or two. Keep your touch light and stay on the tip of the brush. Keep your light source in mind.

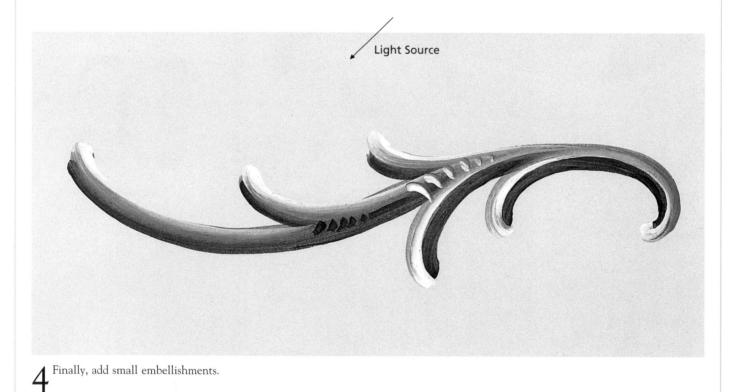

Light Source

4 Finally, add small embellishments.

Painting Folk Art Flowers With Enid Hoessinger

Light Source

Note how the light source is consistent throughout the design: All highlights fall on the same side, and all shadows fall on the same side.

Close-up of the finished box.

Pattern is at 100%

Painting Folk Art Flowers With Enid Hoessinger

Carnation Temptation

his design is extracted from the corner of the schrank's door panels (page 7). With all the scrollwork, the design could easily be overdone. Therefore I've balanced the color throughout the design: The carnations and scrolls are linked with the gold tones; the mini-roses and tulips share the color carried by the daisy centers, creating a soft appearance. The white daisies further tame the overall appearance. Prepare and basecoat the project as described on pages 54–55 and transfer the pattern from pages 124 and 125, as shown on page 56.

Paint the scrolls first, and then the foliage. Adding TW to the mix softens the foliage color. The TW is held face down for all the rose leaves. For tendrils, the MFC is thinned slightly, and the brush is held perpendicular. (Refer to chapter four for procedure.) Next paint the carnations and the tulip. These are budlike and narrow (refer to project three). Paint the mini-roses next. Load the brush in the suggested color and choose any of the roses illustrated in project four. Good control of loading and application is important because of their size. Finish with small, soft white daisies using brushstroke three. Load the daisy brush in white, and then gently sweep a little CC. Start at the back and work toward the front, white side down, replacing the colors as necessary. For the lightest petals, tip with TW and hold it toward the ceiling. The center is a triple load in MTC.

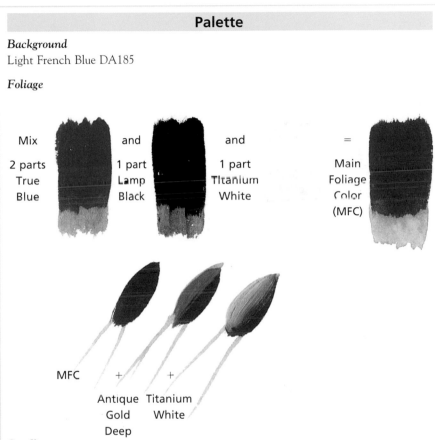

Palette

Background
Light French Blue DA185

Foliage

Mix 2 parts True Blue and 1 part Lamp Black and 1 part Titanium White = Main Foliage Color (MFC)

MFC + Antique Gold Deep + Titanium White

Scrolls
Mix 6 parts Antique Gold Deep and 1 part Burnt Umber and 2 parts Titanium White + Burnt Umber + Titanium White

Tulips
Mix 1 part Brilliant Red and 1 part Burnt Umber (MTC) + Antique Gold Deep + Titanium White

Mini-Roses
Same as the tulips

Carnations
Antique Gold Deep + MTC + Titanium White

Small Daisies
Mix Antique Green and Lamp Black and Titanium White (CC) + Titanium White

SCROLLS

Mixing AGD, BU and TW makes these scrolls slightly softer to complement the soft blue background. Block all scrolls out in this scroll mix, and then follow the instructions below and on pages 113–114. Highlights are added by double-loading in AGD + TW, while shadows are painted with a double load of AGD + BU. Try not to overload the brush and reload both colors as required, in proportion to the strokes.

1 Load the brush in the scroll mix. Start in the center of the shell, blocking out the upper shell quickly with vertical strokes.

2 While still wet, sweep back through BU (do this for every stroke) and work short strokes for the shadows with gold face down. Block out the scroll.

3 Triple-load the already double-loaded brush by tipping with white and paint small turn-backs. Clean the brush. Paint the shadow side of the scroll in a double load with BU, reloading both colors when needed.

4 Tip the brush with TW for the highlights. Keep the white to the inside of the stroke.

Painting Folk Art Flowers With Enid Hoessinger

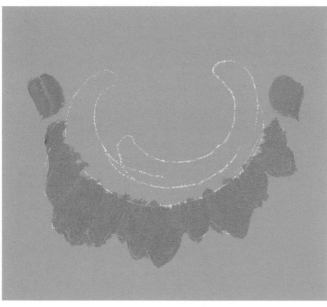

5 Block out the lower shell.

6 While still wet, double-load with BU. Pull multiple short strokes away from the center. Clean the brush. Block the scroll out in scroll mix.

7 Double-load with TW and pull short strokes from the outside. Clean the brush. Double-load with BU and paint the shadow side of the scroll.

8 With tipped TW, paint turn-backs. Increase TW and highlight the scroll. Clean the brush. With thinned BU only, paint the shadows underneath the shell.

CARNATIONS

Golden-toned carnations carry the
tulip and rose color.

1 Mix a touch of MTC and AGD and thin with water. Use this as a wash for the first layer of petals by painting brushstroke ten in a cone shape.

2 Increase AGD + TW. Start working from the light side of the petal.

3 To darken, sweep through the darker color and work from the dark side of the petal.

4 Petals are layered alternately, increasing the gold and white.

5 At this stage, clean the brush and continue in AGD and TW for the petals in front. Note the slight S-stroke on some petals to give them a little character. Add the calyx—it is painted like a small tulip with a triple load of foliage color

6 Finished carnation with supporting foliage and a section of scroll.

©1998

Enlarge pattern to 117% for actual size.

Painting Folk Art Flowers With Enid Hoessinger

All Hung Up

The delightful hanging festoons decorating the sides of the schrank's door panels (page 7) are perfect on this towel stand. Scrolls help to fill the area and provide an element from which the flowers can hang. This project introduces another method of painting leaves, which involves creating veins at the same time. Prepare and basecoat the project as described on pages 54–55 and transfer the pattern from pages 130 and 131, as shown on page 56. Paint the scrolls and foliage first, and then paint the pink roses, referring to project four: For the center, mix with a little MFC to darken. Increase TW to create a very light rose. Paint the tulips next, referring to project three: Load the brush in AGD and sweep through TW multiple times. Push the white well into the brush and sweep gently through a little MRC. Next paint the smaller rose trio, using the suggested colors: Refer to the mini-roses in project four as a guide, but make them somewhat larger. To paint the crocus, mix TB and LB. Roll the excess paint off and wipe the brush on a paper towel. Double-load with TW, sweeping several times. Strike back, holding white down, and paint bold brushstrokes one, two and three to quickly complete this flower.

Palette

Background
Grey Sky DA111

Scrolls
Light French Blue DA185 + mixture of 2 parts Burnt Umber and 1 part True Blue (CC) + Titanium White

Foliage

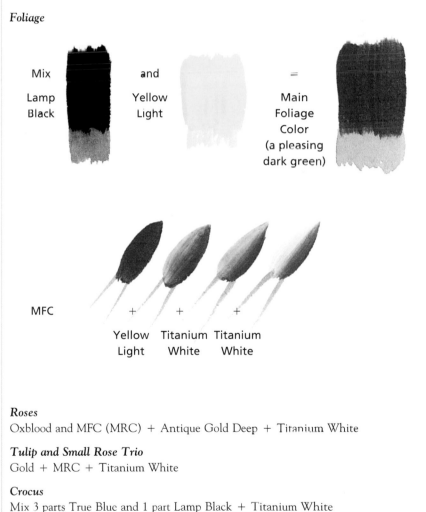

Mix Lamp Black and Yellow Light = Main Foliage Color (a pleasing dark green)

MFC + Yellow Light + Titanium White + Titanium White

Roses
Oxblood and MFC (MRC) + Antique Gold Deep + Titanium White

Tulip and Small Rose Trio
Gold + MRC + Titanium White

Crocus
Mix 3 parts True Blue and 1 part Lamp Black + Titanium White

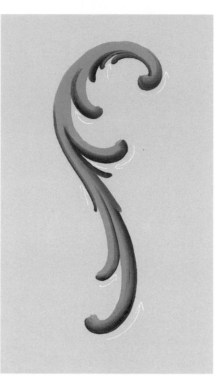

1 Block the scrolls in with Light French Blue, as for project five. This time use a little more pressure to create width.

2 Change to a no. 4 brush and load with Light French Blue. Double-load with CC and paint all the shadows of the scrolls, with the Light French Blue side of the brush to the Light French Blue side of the scroll and the CC to the underside.

3 Clean the brush and reload in Light French Blue. Double-load with TW for the light side of the scrolls, directing the TW to the inside curve of every stroke.

To paint the straight lines, mask off the sides with masking tape. Block the lines in with Light French Blue. With an ox-hair lettering brush, shade the side of the straight lines with CC.

FOLIAGE

1 Mix a little Lamp Black into a puddle of Yellow Light until a medium-dark color is obtained. Roll the excess paint off the brush and paint the darkest leaves as follows: Flatten the brush and, starting at the base of the leaf, paint numerous narrow brushstroke tens lying next to one another. This will leave a trail of veinlike strokes behind. Complete all darkest leaves, creating a balance as you do. Refer to page 37 for tips on loading a knife edge for these leaves.

2 Double-load with Yellow Light and hold the brush so that both colors are visible. Lay these strokes next to one another, walking (see page 51) toward the light and tapering for the shape of the rose leaf. Reload the brush with a little dark on the dark side and light on the light side and walk toward the dark on the brush. Walking away from the dark yields a darker result; walking away from the light yields a lighter result. Study the examples and paint the foliage—dark, medium, and then lightest leaves—in the walking manner.

3 Small rose leaves are painted in a triple load, using brushstroke ten in single strokes with the white side down.

4 Finally, add the washes for shadow foliage.

Close-up of finished flowers.

Bottom half. Enlarge pattern to 168% for actual size.

All Hung Up

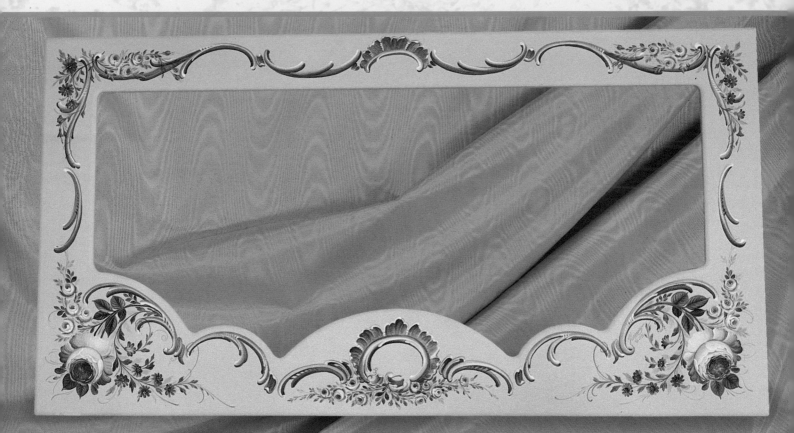

Rococo Elegance

This frame will show you how the designs from the schrank on page 7 can be used to follow curves as well as straight lines, creating a totally different look. Extract the portion of the design required for your article—this design is inspired by the top and bottom motifs on the door panels. Another idea is to use a corner motif for a place mat, with or without scrolls. For the latter, I recommend that a background technique be used as an anchor or filler.

Prepare and basecoat the project as described on pages 54–55 and transfer the pattern from page 139 as shown on page 56. Paint the scrolls first, and then the foliage. As you advance, you may be ready for another challenge, so I have included a special treatment to create rose leaves—the difference is in the veining. Try this method to give a more realistic appearance to your foliage. If these leaves are too difficult, revert back to a technique you feel comfortable with. Next paint the large roses: With MRC in the brush, triple-load with gold and white. Refer to project one for the roses, and to project four for the skirts. Finish with the mini-roses, buds and blue daisies.

Palette

Background
Eggshell DA153

Scrolls
Antique Gold Deep + Burnt Umber + Titanium White

Foliage

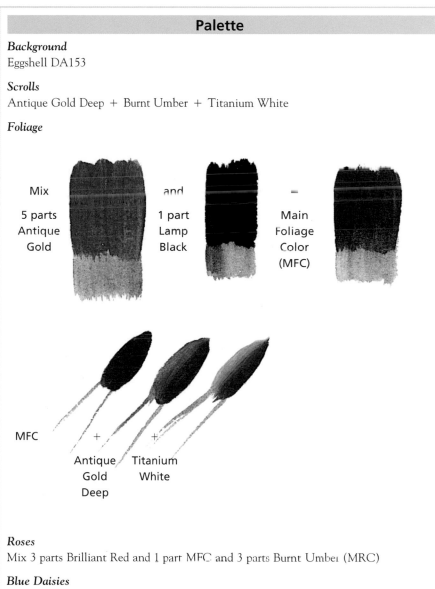

Mix

5 parts Antique Gold

and

1 part Lamp Black

=

Main Foliage Color (MFC)

MFC

+ Antique Gold Deep

+ Titanium White

Roses
Mix 3 parts Brilliant Red and 1 part MFC and 3 parts Burnt Umber (MRC)

Blue Daisies
Mix 2 parts True Blue and 1 part MFC + Titanium White

SCROLLS

Start with the scrolls, referring to project five and the illustrations below.

1 Block the shell out in vertical strokes using AGD.

2 Double-load with a little BU. Lay shadows in with gold face down. Block out the scroll.

3 Paint in the shadows for the scrolls.

4 Tip the double-loaded brush with TW to cap. Increase TW for highlight on scrolls.

Note how the layers, separated here, fit into each other. All scrolls are structured in this manner.

FOLIAGE

This is an advanced technique of foliage painting, and requires practice. I call it the strike-back method.

1 Start by blocking out selected leaves in MFC. Double-load, completing all foliage for the daisies with brushstrokes eight, nine and ten. Triple-load with a little TW and paint the rose leaves primarily using brushstroke ten with the light side down, creating indirect light. No white should be visible.

2 Paint the leaves in single or double loads.

3 When dry, triple-load the brush and then sweep back over MFC. Keeping the white down, use slight pressure to pull the stroke in an even width from the center to the outside of each leaf. Because of the sweep-back, each stroke will start with a dark tip, and by repeating this sweep back action *every time*, the center of the leaf will become dark. When there is a need to lighten up in the center, a strike-back over the palette will be sufficient, and progressively the color will become exhausted on the brush, thus causing a fade-out of color, which is what we want. Walk one way only, either from the tip to the back or vice versa.

5 Add the washes for the balance of the foliage.

4 To indicate the back of a leaf, merely use the general method of knife-edge strokes in light veins. Practice this until you understand the concept. For more light, sweep through the AGD several times, and then several times through the TW, before striking/sweeping back.

MINI-ROSES AND BUDS

Use the same colors as for the large roses. Refer to project four and develop your roses accordingly.

1 Paint the rose mouth with a tight brushstroke thirteen in a triple load.

2 Follow up with strokes wrapped tightly around.

3 Paint the skirts with brushstroke thirteen. While still in a triple load, strike back in MRC and paint short brushstroke threes without tails, white held down, for the buds. The calyx are done in the same manner with the foliage color. The sepals are small brushstrokes one and two on either side and brushstroke three in the middle.

4 Finished mini-roses with buds and supporting foliage.

1 Use a daisy brush (a brush with a worn-off tip) and block the center out in blue.

2 While wet, immediately double-load with TW, face it down and paint the petals until the brush needs reloading.

3 Strike back on the dark side for the balance of petals.

4 The dark center only requires tiny dots of double load in AGD and TW. The calyx is done in foliage color, with small commas for sepals.

Enlarge pattern to 154% for actual size.

Chapter Ten

Finishing Your Work

Patina refers to a discoloration or coating that appears on a surface after years of aging. Very old furniture takes on a dark appearance caused by dust, soot and everyday handling. This antique look is sought after in some decorative arts. We use the patina (or antique) method to give newly painted articles an aged effect. Once the decoration is complete, assess whether you would like to add an aged look to your article using the patina treatment.

Finishing Without Patina

If you don't wish to add an antique finish, be sure to erase all tracing lines with water or a little patina oil (see right) on a cloth over a finger. Use a little diluted detergent to wash any oiliness away. Your surface is then ready to be sealed with a reliable spray sealer or water-based varnish.

Finishing With Patina

If you wish to add a patina effect, leave the tracing lines on—the friction of the eraser will create a slick surface and the patina will not adhere, resulting in a blotchy finish. Many different mediums can be used to create a patina look; however, the old-fashioned method I refer to as the *artists' oil paint* method is my favorite. This method involves applying oil paint to the surface and using "patina oil" as a vehicle. Please feel free to use your own method—you will know the results you wish to achieve.

To prepare the patina oil, mix 1 part refined linseed oil and 4 parts pure gum turps. Slightly thin your oil paint (Burnt Umber) with a little patina oil. Spread the oil paint mix over the entire surface and into crevices using a bristle brush. With a cloth, immediately rub back over the surface in a circular motion, starting in the center of the piece and applying pressure. Gradually release pressure as you work outward. If the effect is too dark, repeat the rubbing back with a little patina oil on a clean piece of cloth. When you have achieved the look you desire, spray it with a sealer—it will be ready to handle after ten minutes. (If you use a brush-on varnish, you will have to let it dry for a minimum of forty-eight hours.) My choice of sealer is DecoArt Matte sealer or a crystal clear sealer. I prefer a satin finish, rather than a glossy look, for wooden articles: This is a matter of personal choice.

Starting in the center, rub patina away with a soft cloth.

The finished project, without patina.

The finished project with patina applied.

Safety Tips

- Turps is highly flammable, and the fumes are hazardous. Read the precautions on the bottle carefully.
- Always close the patina oil bottle, even while you're working, to cut down on fumes and prevent spills.
- Allow sufficient ventilation (use a mask if you wish) and use gloves.
- Spread newspaper down to work on.
- Use lint-free cloths. When finished, drown them and the paper in water prior to disposal. Given the right circumstances they could ignite.

Chapter Eleven

The History of European Folk Art

During the Middle Ages, decorative works were reserved for the church and for articles of the sacraments, as it was not seen fit for "common folk" to become bloated with pride of possession. The style of work done at this time almost certainly stemmed from illuminated manuscripts.

Eventually, toward the end of the Middle Ages, extracts of these designs were painted on walls and panels. This era is known as the early Renaissance or as a transitional period—a period of religious turmoil in which the "folk" became enlightened. One result was that they began to take art into their own hands. During this time, many people fled to other parts of the world, taking their skills with them. Fine craftsmen and artists were sought after and commissioned to manufacture furniture and decor for the courts. Out of necessity, the folk made utensils and naive furniture to meet their needs, sometimes decorating them. This is the most obvious starting point for European decorative painting.

Renaissance

In the late sixteenth and seventeenth centuries, furniture designers traveled to other parts of Europe to keep up with trends set by the courts of Italy and France. The invention of printed designs during the mid-fifteenth century gave tradesmen access to patterns that were particularly useful for carving and marquetry. Reputable craftsmen were called upon to make furniture for castles. Motifs—chiefly inspired by Italy—moved from Gothic through to Classical, incorporating architectural, geometrical and symmetrical designs to soften the arabesques and floral motifs characteristic of the Italian Renaissance.

Meanwhile, village craftsmen saw an opportunity to make furniture affordable to the folk by using "inferior" (soft) woods. To copy the look of the more expensive hardwoods, some innovative craftsmen, particularly in the southern part of Germany, stenciled designs onto their furniture to create an inlaid (marquetry) effect. Decoration began as merely an embellishment to conceal the knots and imperfections of softwoods.

Craftsmen had to be resourceful in making their own painting mediums; for example, one recipe called for soot and ox blood to yield a black-brown color. This color was used for bold motifs of geometric design that developed into floral motifs stenciled onto raw wood. Another popular medium made from glue and wheat starch was known as *kleister*. This clear glue was colored with various earth pigments and stains extracted by boiling nutshells. These earth colors were applied to the entire surface of the furniture pieces, creating special effects and imitating expensive wood grain, marble and other decorative patterns. The common folk also applied this type of decoration to their own handmade furniture, with a lesser degree of accuracy, and added their own ideas to it, which contributed richly to the development of folk art.

Baroque

In the seventeenth to mid-eighteenth centuries, court craftsmen used exotic veneer of various kinds of wood for intricate floral marquetry. These articles bore a likeness to Flemish, Dutch and English floral paintings. Embellishments were rich, and much gilding was used. This era brought about rather formal, exaggerated classical lines, and interior decoration went through many changes, becoming extravagant (and a bit over the top). Furniture painters, in keeping with the fashions of the court, painted furniture for the bourgeoisie bearing evidence of these elaborate designs. Colorful motifs were painted on white panels, and then an aging process (patina) was used to turn the panels ivory. While all this was happening, the folk did not change the symmetry of their designs—they merely introduced color.

By this time, specific regions were incorporating religious symbols in their floral motifs. This style of painting was recognized by the government of the day as *Folk Art* and identified as *Bauernmalerei* in German-speaking regions. A standard was set for such painted furniture: It was important to cover the wood with a colored surface, upon which designs were painted. Whether this was to conceal the busy grain of "inferior" wood or to preserve it from vermin, it certainly set a precedent for decorated furniture in Germany—decoration in color required a painted background.

Rococo

During the mid-eighteenth century fashion changed again—and so did furniture. The rococo style originated in France, but caught on very quickly all over Europe. It had a tremendous impact in Germany, Switzerland and Austria, although the style varied from country to country. The courts, in particular, welcomed the change because the rococo style added an air of sophistication, elegance and romance. This style opened up opportunities for new designs and more delicate construction. During this era—which was relatively peaceful, particularly in France—the desire of the courts and aristocrats to be surrounded by luxury spelled prosperity for the common people. The bourgeoisie welcomed the change, particularly in Germany and America: As furniture became less elaborate and more practical, it became more affordable.

Typical features of the rococo style are the repetitive curves in C and S shapes, called *rocailles* (rockwork), or commonly known as *scrolls*. These were no longer organic, as in the classical form, but a deliberate break away, with more delicate and casual lines than the shapes of the Baroque era, creating a livelier, romantic mood. Along with these scrolls, the demand was for light backgrounds and an abundance of naturalistic flowers.

These designs were used for carving and had a tendency to become overloaded with detail. While scrolls were mostly used as an embellishment, the placement was designed to add strength or support. Porcelain mounts with painted scenes were the order of the day.

Given the growing affluence of the bourgeoisie, homes improved and windows became larger, so the dark, strong colors of the past were no longer desirable. Lighter and brighter colors became the trend.

Delicate designs of flowers entwined with three-dimensional shells and rockwork emerged. Imagination was given free rein. Urns with elaborate handles of intricate scrollwork, holding pastel, naturalistic flowers in abundance, sometimes overloaded one piece, with scrolled borders and marbled effects on surrounds, friezes and plinths. Wonderful examples of this style can be found in museums, and they provide great inspiration for folk artists today. Naturally, according to our lifestyle and taste for decor, we can add as little or as much as we would like.

This must have been a very exciting time for painters, as the previous era did not give them many new designs to work with, other than the strap work—still in wood tones—or bold colors applied in a stencil-like manner. With asymmetrical form, freedom of design and a lot of resource material to work with, these craftsmen were able to express their capabilities.

At this time, the demand for painted furniture was increasing. Commissions were personalized by series of paintings that recorded events in the customer's life. Panels might all depict religious themes, or saints could be painted in upper panels and vases of flowers in lower panels. Some professional furniture painters had

workshops set up to produce the furniture and also employed decorators. Examples of this work (generally on wardrobes) is most evident in books; this work often takes the name of a particular workshop, of the region or of the master furniture painter. The repetition of design usually is a giveaway. Marbled plinths and friezes were featured.

In contrast, a tradition emerged among the folk of the land: painting as a way of recording history. Painted panels depicted faiths, lifestyles, possessions, occupations and hobbies, almost like a photo album. The seasons were strikingly used in allegories. As professional furniture painters observed furniture trends, the folk of the land observed the new forms coming into vogue. They were slow to change, as they had already established a regional style, but new influences continued to mold it. I would say that the elements of this era were simply too good to ignore—scrollwork has been featured prominently from its arrival right up to the present. The folk frequently combined styles incorrectly, in ignorance, yet the result was charming, with childlike naiveté. In the early years of my research, this factor confused me as I tried to establish styles relating to the eras.

The folk passed their designs from one generation to the next, which contributed to a style or motif becoming characteristic of a particular region. Evolutionary changes came about with the eras; looking back, one can trace this evolution. Today, especially, this factor is highly valued in the respective regions as part of their heritage. Any change at all would have been frowned upon. Museums display these articles with pride as the folklore of their local regions. Frequently, one will find that articles belonging to one region will appear elsewhere, most likely as a result of traveling salesmen or marriage between people from different regions. Often the future husband may have been the painter. Sometimes it is difficult to establish the origin of such work, as the folk did not necessarily put their mark on it.

Although the folk were committed to painting their own traditional motifs in regional style, it is evident that individuals recorded their own interpretations and expressions. This could be as little as a name or a quip, but could also be as much as allegoric pictures representing, naively or artistically, an event of some importance.

Empire

This era lasted from 1797 to 1814. Soon after the death of Louis XV, the Neoclassic style was adopted in France, during the time of the Directorate (*Directoire*); however, in Germany, court furnishers still worked in a developed rococo style as late as the 1770s. With the Neoclassic style (Louis Seize) barely accepted in Germany, the Empire style (during the reign of Napoleon) readily found favor by the Germans. This style became less clumsy than its forerunner, with a strong influence of English and French design, and found favor on an international scale.

As in previous cases, Empire painted furniture bore witness to its time. Tall urns of formal floral arrangements defined the elegance and formality that became the signature of the era. Typical subjects were soldiers and elegantly dressed couples. The master painters of this time, again inspired by furniture fashion, had an opportunity to explore lavish design. Painted furniture was in demand, and no longer stood in as an alternative to the real thing. Some artists went to extremes; others maintained design

simplicity. This, together with the demands of the customer, indicates a gradual change during this period of affluence.

Styles in a given region still differed dramatically, bearing traces of particular eras and often even a combination of several. This aspect came about as a result of individuals traveling, bringing ideas and cultures from other regions into their work. African wild animals and indigenous people featured in design indicate these phenomena. Saints and people depicted in allegoric settings are typical of the time, as are cultivated and exotic flowers. Interestingly enough, field flowers were never featured in these designs.

Regional differences always applied, but colors were largely in soft tones and wood grain. In some cases, designs from the Renaissance and the Baroque eras were combined on these light colors, which is indicative of

individualism.

Again, the folk did not much care if they adhered to the style of the present. By this time, styles characteristic of their region, frequently with religious themes, were well established. Apart from periodic additions of the relevant era, most likely copied from furniture they saw, this work was not easy to date, as was the master furniture painters' work.

Biedermeier

After years of France dominating furniture fashion, with other countries following suite, Viennese craftsmen who worked in the French style adapted the Empire style, setting a new trend in furniture, popular from 1815 to 1830, that became known as *Biedermeier*. For the first time in history, furniture design became practical and served a purpose for everyday comfortable living. Pieces included functional round tables and chairs,

secretaries, Biedermeier sofas, ladies' sewing boxes and casual tables—all creating a warm, homey atmosphere. In Austria and southern Germany, lighter woods such as fruit woods, birch, elm and the like were preferred; northern Germany, England and France still preferred the darker colors. The practical, comfortable and simpler lines of the Biedermeier style were readily accepted, in particular by the German-speaking middle class impoverished by civil wars.

Furniture classified as true Biedermeier was not cluttered by decoration, but emphasized natural wood grain, fine and rare burlwood veneer and inlays. This was true of furniture produced until 1830, after which elements of bygone eras again reappeared and combined, embellishing the simplicity of Biedermeier, which was eventually referred to as a "culmination of eras."

The same held true for painted furniture during this era. Very few pieces were really as uncluttered as one might think, and all too soon the painted-furniture trade experienced the same fate—incorrect combinations (apart from a few examples from Switzerland) painted in the darker colors, with floral design restricted to a posy or a garland. More evident would have been the paintings in panels, which reflected the affluence, lifestyle and comfort of the people.

Humor in Folk Art A variety of utensils and articles decorated during this time reflected a great sense of humor. This is evident in the painting from an ardent lover, recording erotic design and quips on bentwood boxes, generally regarded as a "wedding box." (It must have become a trend after one particularly witty and risqué lover painted a piece.) The old German writing style was the only thing protecting the meaning from being obvious.

Besides the influence on furniture, this era had a great impact on general lifestyle. It became evident that individuals were looking after themselves. Standards of living were raised, and time was taken to appreciate companionship and the family, as well as beautiful things like fine art and crafts, fashion and accessories. Two poets, Mr. Biedermann and Mr. Bummelmeier, contributed to the naming of this epoch—Biedermeier.

The Decline and Rebirth of Folk Art

At the dawn of the mechanical era, most decoration was replaced by lithographs, with isolated pieces of furniture painted toward the middle of the nineteenth century. Development of the art form ceased with the Biedermeier era. Decorated furniture became crude and unwanted. Those who could afford to replaced it with modern furniture, and others ruthlessly painted over it.

It was a century later when, as a result of wars and poverty, these socalled unwanted pieces of furniture were uncovered from attics and barns, and historians realized the wealth of their heritage. They started to research the origins in earnest and collectors snapped the pieces up over the following decades (up to the present day, in fact). Since the 1950s, workshops have been springing up all over Europe—and further afield—in an attempt to revive these treasures of the past. I feel privileged to be a part of this revival.

Painting Folk Art Flowers With Enid Hoessinger